The Real Gatsby

The Real Gatsby:
GEORGE GORDON MOORE

A Granddaughter's Memoir

Mickey Rathbun

White River Press
Amherst, Massachusetts

Copyright © 2024 by Sheila Blair Rathbun
All rights reserved.

Published by White River Press
Amherst, MA 01004 • www.whiteriverpress.com

ISBN: 979-8-88545-003-4

Book and Cover Design by Douglas Lufkin, Lufkin Graphic Designs
Norwich, VT 05055 • www.lufkingraphics.com

Library of Congress Cataloging-in-Publication Data

Names: Rathbun, Sheila Blair, 1955- author.
Title: The real Gatsby George Gordon Moore : a granddaughter's memoir / Mickey Rathbun.
Description: Amherst : White River Press, [2024]
Identifiers: LCCN 2023036254 | ISBN 9798885450034 (trade paperback)
Subjects: LCSH: Moore, George Gordon, 1875-1971. | Gatsby, Jay (Fictitious character) | Rathbun, Sheila Blair, 1955- | Moore family.
Classification: LCC CT275.M5935 R38 2024 | DDC 809--dc23/eng/20230816
LC record available at https://lccn.loc.gov/2023036254

For Chris, Tommy, and Nicholas with love

Contents

Prologue: A Photograph and a Jar of Sand i

Chapter 1: Dauntless Centaurs 1

Chapter 2: The Real Gatsby? 7

Chapter 3: Wyoming 14

Chapter 4: Gaining Traction 19

Chapter 5: The Racing Life 26

Chapter 6: "I Discovered England" 32

Chapter 7: Hunting Pigs in Paradise 37

Chapter 8: Cowboy and Cotton 44

Chapter 9: London Calling 56

Chapter 10: Looks, Bloodlines, and Money 65

Chapter 11: "War is Certain. Come at Once." 74

Chapter 12: A Mother's Meddling 86

Chapter 13: Dances of Death 98

Chapter 14: A Fog of Ignorance and Doubt 102

Chapter 15: A German Spy at GHQ? 115

Chapter 16: "I Always Fear What Too Many Know" . . 125
Chapter 17: Reckonings 131
Chapter 18: The Governor's Daughter 138
Chapter 19: The Golden State 144
Chapter 20: Stanway on the Pacific 150
Chapter 21: A 23,000-Acre Playground 160
Chapter 22: Empty Promises 166
Chapter 23: Childhood at Rancho San Carlos 169
Chapter 24: The Foss Twins Behave Badly 178
Chapter 25: Decline and Fall 186
Chapter 26: "My Easter Holidays" 195
Chapter 27: Orphans 202
Chapter 28: Out Stealing Horses 210
Chapter 29: Ending Up 218
Chapter 30: Rancho San Carlos Revisited 226

Epilogue: How the Ranch Was Lost 233

Acknowledgments 243
Notes on Sources 245
Illustration Credits 259
About the Author 263

— PROLOGUE —

A Photograph and a Jar of Sand

MY HUSBAND AND I were married in the foothills of the Blue Ridge Mountains, the heart of Virginia horse country, nearly 40 years ago. It was early October; fall colors were beginning to glow in the trees, and the countryside smelled of ripening apples and the final hay-cutting of the season. The Piedmont, as this part of Virginia is called, is dotted with stately antebellum houses full of stories and not a few dark secrets. Our wedding reception took place in one such house, called Welbourne, in Middleburg, a few miles from my parents' farm, where I had grown up. A chance encounter on that momentous day inspired my quest to solve the mystery of George Gordon Moore, my maternal grandfather.

Welbourne has been in the same family for eight generations. Some of the descendants still live there; for many years they have operated it as an inn frequented by foxhunting enthusiasts. Built of brick and stuccoed a soft yellow, with tall white columns, the house has an aura of well-worn majesty. Legendary fighters for the slaveholding Confederacy, including Jeb Stuart and John Mosby, are said to have stayed at Welbourne during the Civil War, and many illustrious guests have visited there since.

Chris and I had spent our two-year courtship mostly in Boston, where he was in graduate school, and New York, where I had recently embarked on a legal career. For us, the rural southern wedding was a lark, a pleasant detour into a genteel world where time seemed to move more slowly, if it moved at all. Guests nibbled country-ham biscuits and drank champagne and Kentucky bourbon out on the veranda. Late roses and pale hydrangeas, rouged like old ladies' cheeks, still bloomed in the gardens; as darkness fell, I glimpsed a few couples wandering in the overgrown boxwood maze behind the house.

Among the guests were my mother's cousin Honoria Donnelly and her husband, Bill, two of my parents' oldest and dearest friends. Honoria was the daughter of Gerald and Sara Murphy, the celebrated expatriate couple at the center of F. Scott Fitzgerald's coterie. The Donnellys had booked a room at the same rustic inn where Chris and I were spending our wedding night. When we arrived there after the reception we ran into them at the front desk. Although it was nearly midnight, Bill and Honoria insisted on toasting our future with a nightcap. He ordered a bottle of champagne, and we sat in the empty bar trading family stories. With her pearly skin and halo of silvery blonde hair, Honoria seemed as effervescent as the champagne we sipped. She told us how much she had enjoyed the wedding. "Did you know that Scott Fitzgerald stayed at Welbourne?" she asked.

Chris had just gotten his Ph.D. in American literature and was intrigued to hear that Fitzgerald had stayed in the very house where we had cut our wedding cake. I mentioned that my grandfather had also stayed at Welbourne during his annual Christmas visits many years earlier. "George Gordon Moore," she murmured. "He was a colorful character."

While I knew only sketchy details of my grandfather's life, I had heard it mentioned that he had been F. Scott Fitzgerald's model for Jay Gatsby. As a teenager I had loved *The Great Gatsby* although I could not fully grasp its moral ambiguity. The story about Gatsby and my grandfather had lodged in my brain. But as far as I could tell, neither my mother nor anyone else in the family took it seriously. That evening in Virginia, as we sat with Honoria and Bill talking about weddings and F. Scott Fitzgerald, the Gatsby story floated into my mind. I wondered whether, having grown up with the Fitzgeralds, Honoria might know something about the speculation regarding my grandfather and Gatsby. In that champagne-addled moment I mentioned the story about Fitzgerald and my grandfather and asked her if she thought it might be true. She raised her eyebrows and smiled her ethereal smile. "It wouldn't surprise me at all," she said. She may have been trying to humor me, or perhaps she'd had one too many glasses of champagne. But I went to sleep on my wedding night puzzling over the possibility that my grandfather might have been the inspiration for Jay Gatsby, one of the most famous characters in American literature.

And yet, during the days and years that followed, it was difficult for me to imagine any connection between the dapper Jay Gatsby and the shabby old man who had visited our family every year at Christmas. He was aloof, without a trace of the coziness that I saw in other people's grandparents. My siblings—Gordon and Jennie—and I called him "Grandfather" and kept a wary distance. Old age had not been kind to him. His eyes were milky blue and his ears were as long as a bloodhound's. He combed his stringy white hair across his scalp with sweet-smelling tonic. He was already eighty years old when I was born and he died at ninety-six, so I knew him only during the last years of his life. I understood that he lived in an apartment in Los Angeles and had so little money that my parents sent him plane tickets for his annual visit. His diminished circumstances made me wonder what had gone wrong.

The Real Gatsby

Gordon, Jennie, and I with our grandfather (me on his lap), July 1959

My parents owned a few racehorses, and when my grandfather visited we would go to the local Middleburg training track early in the morning to watch the horses work out. His clothes—a threadbare suit, a double-breasted polo coat, and a brown fedora—were not suitable for our harsh East Coast winters, but he refused my father's offer of a heavy, unstylish overcoat. He carried a stopwatch so that he could clock the horses' half-mile sprints. Every night after dinner he and my parents would sit by the fire drinking brandy and talking about horses.

My grandfather occasionally launched into rheumy recitations of Romantic poetry that bewildered my siblings and me. We exchanged surreptitious glances, stifled giggles, and yearned for a chance to escape. He was particularly fond of the poetry of Byron, a man known for his grand aristocratic gestures, enormous debts, and infamous love affairs. His parents may well have named him after George Gordon, Lord Byron, in keeping with the intense surge of

A Photograph and a Jar of Sand

"Byronomania" during the nineteenth century. In any case, as I would discover much later, his life certainly echoed the great poet's in its flamboyant excesses.

I remember sitting at the dinner table on Christmas Eve when my father served his special oyster stew, ceremoniously prepared with fresh oysters from Virginia's Eastern Shore and quarts of heavy cream and butter. This was a yearly ritual I dreaded. The sight and smell of the oysters repelled me; their curled gray bodies reminded me of my grandfather's pendulous ears. I crumbled handfuls of oyster crackers into my bowl and stirred them around. Watching my grandfather consume this dish nearly made me gag. Each slurped spoonful sent a trickle of creamy broth down the old man's chin and onto his shirtfront. I imagined bits of chewed oyster nesting in the nooks of his knitted woolen tie.

Despite his straitened circumstances, I was dimly aware that much earlier in his life—long before the ghastly Christmas Eve dinners—my grandfather had been a very rich and powerful man. I knew that he had once owned the enormous Rancho San Carlos in Carmel, California, where my mother and her brother, David, one year her junior, lived until their parents separated in 1931.

My mother had never said much about her father's life. But she did tell us that he had lost the fabled ranch in the Great Depression. She said that he could have saved the property but he had been too proud to accept the offer from his ex-wife—my grandmother—to pay off the mortgage. My mother seemed resolute about this loss. But I realized later that she had been devastated by it.

My mother was an alcoholic, and it was only when she was drunk that she talked about her childhood, which had been marred by her parents' marital infidelities, divorces, and financial problems. She veered from fond recollections of the two neighboring ranches in Carmel where she had grown up, to torrents of bitterness and rage aimed not only at her heedless, self-involved parents but at everyone in our family. She often told a nightmarish story about finding her favorite horses in the barn dead from colic. A careless stable hand had left the feed-room door open and the horses had literally gorged themselves to death. In her drunken rants she sometimes hinted that she might shoot our horses and maybe even our dogs. This was no idle threat. She kept a .22 rifle in the house in case an animal was seriously injured and needed to be put down.

When my mother was sober, she was brilliant, clever, and funny. But her alcoholic outbursts terrified me. I never dared to stray into the minefield of her past. It might as well have been roped off with yellow caution tape.

Knowing as little as I did of my grandfather, my impression of him crystallized around two things in our house: a photograph that hung in our living room and a jar of sand. To me, these distinctive objects were the bookends of his mysterious life.

The photograph was a framed enlargement of a 1928 newspaper picture captioned "Great Polo Players at Del Monte," a reflection of my grandfather's erstwhile glory. It shows him dressed in jodhpurs and boots, standing in front of a stable in Pebble Beach with three other horsemen, all casually attired in tweed. The men have doffed their hats and have polo mallets close at hand. The caption identifies them as members of the Rancho San Carlos Cardinals polo team. To my grandfather's left is Aidan Roark, a suave polo player from Ireland. He is the most nattily dressed of the group, sporting a diamond-patterned vest, a bold tie, and a silk handkerchief in his breast pocket. His slicked-back hair glistens with pomade. He was to complicate my grandparents' lives soon enough. Standing next to Roark is Averell Harriman, heir to one of America's biggest Gilded Age fortunes. He is tall and slender, with the classically bland good looks of an aristocrat. He grew up playing polo and went on to be a renowned banker, politician, and statesman. The fourth teammate, Tommy Hitchcock, was born into a prominent New York family of horsemen. He is considered the greatest American polo player of all time. He poses jauntily for the camera—one hand in his pocket, his ankles crossed—but his serious expression reflects the world-class athlete he was. Hitchcock, as I would later learn, was the inspiration for several characters in F. Scott Fitzgerald's novels, including Tom Buchanan in *The Great Gatsby*.

Even before I knew who these men were, the photograph radiated their wealth and privilege. I assumed that my grandfather must have enjoyed a similar station in life. But this was just a snapshot of one moment in time. I knew practically nothing about what had come before or what would come after.

"Great Polo Players at Del Monte"

The second object was a jar of coarse gray sand from the Mojave Desert in California. My grandfather had brought it east one Christmas and presented it to my parents as an auspicious talisman. He claimed it was full of valuable minerals that would make him rich again if my parents would finance his project to mine and market it. They evidently rejected my grandfather's proposal. I gathered it was not the first time he had tried to finagle money from them. The jar of sand ended up on the mantelpiece among an assortment of carved jade figurines and silver cigarette boxes. It perplexed me. How could my grandfather get rich by digging up sand? How did he know it was special? My brother said it contained uranium and that we would die instantly if we touched it. The sand appeared to me emblematic of my grandfather. Like the great mysteries of life, it seemed to withhold its secrets. It was enigmatic, full of hope and promise, like a genie in a bottle. But maybe dangerous, too.

My mother died of emphysema in 2005. In the years following her death, I began to explore family territory that she had put off-limits. I had always been curious about my grandfather, the "polo great" who visited us at Christmas bearing a portentous jar of sand. My desire to learn more about this mystifying man was the seed from which this book grew. I had so many questions. I knew he had ended up on the dole, but where had he come from and how had he risen to prominence? How exactly had he lost the ranch? And could he really have been the model for Jay Gatsby?

I pulled on the Gatsby thread first. As I unraveled the particulars of my grandfather's Jazz Age celebrity and his multiple ties to Fitzgerald, I was inevitably drawn into the years that preceded the 1920s and those that followed. It soon became clear that the Gatsby story, as tantalizing as it was, was just one piece of my grandfather's long and astonishing life. He had accomplished many remarkable things on the world stage that my mother had never mentioned. Why the silence? Was the subject of her father too painful to discuss, or were there things that she simply didn't know about?

At first, I approached the subject of my grandfather with detachment. I saw him as an intriguing character who had lived in a world completely removed from mine, like a distant historical figure. The few childhood memories I had of him in his dotage had not forged any sense of personal connection to him. As I puzzled over the Gatsby question, the real man blurred with the fictional character, becoming even more remote. My grandfather seemed to exist not only in another time, but in a world apart from reality. He had nothing to do with me.

I soon realized, however, that he had everything to do with me. This mysterious one-time millionaire was my mother's father, after all. By all accounts my grandfather had been phenomenally intelligent; my mother had certainly inherited his awesome mind. But the more I learned about him, the more I saw how his reckless and negligent behavior had profoundly shaped her. She had grown up in a difficult and unpredictable world where she was often abandoned, emotionally if not physically. She carried that psychic damage into adulthood, nursing it with alcohol and eventually inflicting it on her own children. One generation removed, my siblings and I were also victims of my grandfather's heedless lifestyle. We shared a deep connection to the man that I had earlier failed to comprehend.

What started out as a dispassionate recounting of my grandfather's life became far more complicated and far more personal. I wasn't simply connecting historical dots; I was also examining how my grandfather had influenced my mother, and how that erratic relationship had affected my siblings and me. In the end, this book, which began as an excavation of my grandfather's life, grew into the story of a family and its secrets.

— CHAPTER 1 —

Dauntless Centaurs

M Y GRANDFATHER showed up on Long Island the summer of 1919 with a polo mallet in one hand and a business card in the other. The card read "George Gordon Moore, Capitalist." He was a striking figure, with jet-black hair, intense brown eyes, a dark complexion, and a stocky physique developed by years of training in the boxing gym and, more recently, on the polo field. Moore's trip was more than an opportunity for sporting pleasure. London had been his financial playground before the war, but the war had bled England dry, and New York had usurped London's role as the world's banker. Moore, forty-three at the time, knew there was wealth to be mined on Long Island's North Shore. With its country estates, bucolic meadows, and pristine oceanfront, the North Shore had become a paradise for socialites, celebrities, and well-heeled entrepreneurs in search of glamour and the good life. Long Island was one of those places, as Fitzgerald wrote in *The Great Gatsby*, where "people played polo and were rich together." There was nowhere Moore would rather have been; it was a new piggybank waiting to be cracked.

Moore had had his first taste of polo in 1912 when he was invited to play at the San Mateo Polo Club, just south of San Francisco. It didn't take him longer than a New York minute to realize that polo had all the trappings of wealth and class he coveted. As a 1917 article in *Sunset* magazine put it, "Polo is King in American society and where polo goes Milady and her fleet of trunks go also. In fact, it is considered now part of a debutante's social equipment that she can tell a No. 1 in polo from a Back and will recognize an off-side play." Polo was not just a game, it was a lifestyle.

Emboldened by his time in England during the war, Moore felt he had acquired a sufficient aura of aristocracy to style himself as a polo player. After the Armistice, he headed to California to take up the sport. Years earlier, he had done business with William S. Tevis Jr., scion of a venerable California family and a member of the Santa Barbara Polo Club. Moore reacquainted himself with Tevis, and with Tevis's support and encouragement, he joined the club and threw himself into the sport with fierce determination. A seasoned sports commentator called polo players "dauntless centaurs." The game is fiendishly difficult, involving the coordination of many bodies—human and equine—moving quickly and independently as they try to drive a small, hard white ball into the opponents' goal. Although dangerous and unsportsmanlike conduct is prohibited, polo entails much brute physical contact. As Will Rogers famously remarked, "They call polo a gentleman's game for the same reason that they call a tall man 'Shorty.'"

Short on polo experience but long on money, Moore bankrolled the four-man Santa Barbara squad. In return for his financial backing, Moore was named team captain. Within a few months of his arrival in Santa Barbara, he was in command of one of the West Coast's most successful polo teams. In June 1919, the team and their ponies traveled by train across the country. Their destination was Long Island, New York; their ambition was to dominate the East Coast's summer polo season.

Although polo was relatively new in the West, the Santa Barbara foursome stood strong against the more seasoned eastern teams. At the 1919 Monmouth Cup championship match in Rumson, New Jersey, a highpoint of the East Coast season, Santa Barbara took on the Meadowbrook Polo Club of Westbury, Long Island, the oldest and most prestigious club in the country. Meadowbrook's team that day included C. V. "Sonny" Whitney, an heir to the Whitney and Vanderbilt fortunes, and John Rodman "Roddy" Wanamaker, an heir to the Philadelphia department store empire. But its top player was Tommy Hitchcock, a celebrated young war hero who had just completed his first semester at Harvard. Even in 1919, it was clear that Hitchcock was bound for greatness. He was an extraordinary athlete, combining bravery, cunning, and ruthlessness with grace and humility that gained the respect of every player he faced. Fans and sportswriters idolized him on and off the field. His name was to polo what Babe Ruth's was to baseball.

Both Hitchcock's parents were seasoned equestrians, and young Tommy was swinging a polo mallet from the back of a horse by age six. At twelve, he was sent to St. Paul's School in New Hampshire. From the outbreak of World War I in August 1914, Hitchcock and his family paid close attention to the combat in Europe. Born in France, his mother had close ties there that made the horrors of war especially troubling. When the United States joined the Allies in the spring of 1917, Hitchcock signed on with the celebrated Lafayette Flying Corps, a branch of the French Foreign Legion composed mainly of American aviators. At the time, Hitchcock was seventeen years old and two months shy of his graduation from St. Paul's.

Hitchcock's experience in the war was harrowing and heroic. He flew several successful combat missions before being shot down in German territory, where he was held prisoner for six months. While being moved from one prison camp to another, he jumped off the train and escaped. He made his way on foot, traveling only at night, more than a hundred miles to the safety of the Swiss border. Hitchcock's physical courage and mental toughness captivated America's imagination. Endowed with well-proportioned, aristocratic features and a sturdy, powerful frame, he looked the part of the warrior-athlete. The country, reeling from the trauma of the war, eagerly embraced him. Hitchcock was only nineteen when he played for the Monmouth Cup, but he was already a "newspaper hero," as F. Scott Fitzgerald, a fervent admirer of Hitchcock, put it.

Hitchcock's biographer, Nelson W. Aldrich Jr., compared the 1919 Santa Barbara team to "a band of outlaws let loose in the manicured gardens of the East." They played a rough-and-tumble game that took their gentlemanly competitors by surprise. The West Coast players "were not gentlemen, almost by definition," wrote Aldrich. The Californians knew that Hitchcock was Meadowbrook's secret weapon and they were determined to box him in, whatever it took. From the moment the Monmouth Cup players rode onto the field—the Meadowbrook team in its trademark robin's egg blue and the Santa Barbara players in their all-white jerseys—it was clear that the game would be an epic confrontation between the blue-blooded civility of the East and the red-blooded barbarism of the West.

The competition was ferocious, and Moore was the most ferocious of all. He repeatedly blocked Hitchcock by digging his shoulder into Hitchcock's ribs. At one point, when Hitchcock tried to gallop past him, Moore shouted, "You son of a bitch!" and struck him—perhaps accidentally—on the side of the head with his mallet. A few strides later, Hitchcock realized that the blow had lacerated his ear and that blood was streaming down his shoulder. He left the game long enough to be bandaged up and came back on the field, as Aldrich put it, "not angry with Moore but resolved to give him the roughest three chukkers of polo the older man would ever see."

Santa Barbara defeated Meadowbrook that day. Hitchcock never liked to lose but he was impressed by Moore's ruthless tenacity. Moore likewise admired Hitchcock's unflinching mastery of the sport and his effortless upper-class gentility.

Despite their twenty-five-year age difference, the two competitors became close friends. They continued to play together at Meadowbrook for the rest of the summer. Moore applied himself to the game with doggedness and discipline. Hitchcock appreciated his eagerness to learn and helped him improve his accuracy and teamwork so that he need not rely on physical strength alone. Years later, looking back on that summer, Moore said, "The most important thing I did that year was to play polo with the best team on Long Island."

Like so many other young men who had survived the war, Tommy Hitchcock had returned home feeling aimless, confused. The thrill and danger of battle had exhilarated him; he sought to replicate the authenticity of that experience on the polo field. While some found Moore's brutality on the field offensive, Hitchcock enjoyed it. His bloody clashes with Moore were nothing if not authentic. He had the scars to prove it. He admired the older man's *otherness,* his raw energy and combativeness. For Hitchcock, Moore, a self-made man who followed his passions with force and grit, was the living embodiment of the American Dream.

Moore's latest gambit involved mining metals, a pursuit that sparked Hitchcock's sense of adventure. In the 1920s, "mining lay closer to the heart of the American dream than most enterprises," observed Aldrich. "When Moore was young, mining was still a *frontier* gamble, an outdoorsman's risk: the flash of gold in the pan, the dull gleam of ore in dark tunnels, the gusher in the desert." Imagining a future for himself in Moore's rugged realm of business, Hitchcock studied chemistry at Harvard. Casting about for a job, he was grateful when Moore offered to take him on as his associate. After graduating from Harvard in 1922, Hitchcock began working at Moore's office in midtown Manhattan, learning the intricacies of the minerals trade, speculation, and finance.

The relationship between Hitchcock and Moore epitomized the collision of Old and New Money that was to define the Roaring Twenties. Several years ago, I visited Nelson

Aldrich at his home in Connecticut. He is best known for his book *Old Money: The Mythology of Wealth in America*, an insightful analysis of the relationship between money, social status, and success. Aldrich remembered my grandfather and the outsized role he had played in Hitchcock's early life. In his view, Moore "was a perfect type of the reckless adventurer who had always fascinated Tommy." He suggested that while Moore did not enjoy the privilege of Old Money, he enjoyed the freedom from its rigid rules of conduct. Aldrich saw him as a "buccaneer," ready to overstep the bounds of prudence and decorum when it suited him. As a once-poor immigrant, he had an "edge," said Aldrich. "He did not know what he could not do."

— CHAPTER 2 —

The Real Gatsby?

DURING THE EARLY TWENTIES, Moore lived in a brownstone at 54 East 52nd Street that he shared with Hitchcock and several of his classmates from St. Paul's. Moore's polo-playing friend Averell Harriman, heir to a massive railroad fortune, spent much of his free time there. Although his stodgy patrician background could hardly have been more different from Moore's, Harriman was charmed by his host's spirited extravagance. Moore's townhouse was notorious for its bachelor ambience. Hitchcock did his best to remain above the fray, but John Gaston, one of the St. Paul's roommates, loved to make trouble for him. When Gaston's telephone calls to his lover happened to be answered by the woman's husband or a servant, he would leave Hitchcock's name. Moore recalled that when Gaston was married, his bride jokingly suggested that Moore's housemates were actually "fairies," presumably because they were such close friends. According to Moore, Gaston "laughed himself sick," and told his bride that "if there is any spot in that house, six by four, upstairs or down, where some girl hasn't been laid, I'll eat it."

Even in a decade of conspicuous extravagance, the parties Moore held at his 52nd Street townhouse were renowned. The house featured exotically decorated parlors, including the "Roman" and "Persian" rooms, appropriate for the bacchanals that the house came to be known for. One of Moore's most ardent admirers was the Irish writer Mary Colum, who lived in New York with her husband and fellow writer Padraic Colum. In her memoir, *Life and the Dream,* Colum wrote that "the maddest, merriest of those [Jazz Age] parties, which at the same time managed to be discriminating, were those given by a handsome, wealthy connoisseur of the arts, George Gordon Moore." She observed that champagne flowed freely at Moore's parties: "nothing so vulgar as gin was served." Moore's intellectual firepower was not lost on her. He was "gay, ready-minded, brilliant," she wrote. "He bought whole libraries now and again so as to have something to read when he went to live in a shack by a coal mine or in an adobe hut on a ranch."

Like Gatsby's guests, Colum noted that some of the people who came to Moore's parties had never been invited at all, or had been invited "at second or third remove." She recalled one evening when her husband was seated next to a beautiful young woman and asked Moore who she was. Moore said he didn't know but he encouraged Padraic to find out. She turned out to be a movie actress who, according to Mary, told Padraic that she didn't know anyone at the party. "Tommy Hitchcock brought me here," she said. "Do you mean the polo player?" asked Padraic. "I don't know who he is," replied the woman. "I met him on the train coming from California, and he invited me to the party he was going to."

In Colum's eyes, each of Moore's guests had some special quality. "The women guests, society women, cinema actresses, debutantes, celebrities of some sort, were lovely to look at, or distinguished, and sometimes dazzlingly dressed," she wrote. "The men were most entertaining and appeared to be of every nationality and every shade of opinion. Our host reminded me of a Roman emperor—maybe it was Hadrian—who gave entertaining parties, knew everybody, had been everywhere, including to the wars and the provinces." It's easy to see how Moore might have made a strong impression on a newcomer in that heady milieu.

The Real Gatsby?

In the fall of 1922, F. Scott Fitzgerald and his wife, Zelda, settled in the town of Great Neck on Long Island's North Shore, near the Meadowbrook Polo Club, where Hitchcock and Moore played every weekend. As Fitzgerald wrote to his cousin Cecie, "Great Neck is a great place for celebrities." He had reason to know. Three years earlier, his first novel, *This Side of Paradise,* had received rave reviews, launching him into celebrity in his own right. His play, *The Vegetable,* was to be produced in New York the following November. Despite his newfound fame, Fitzgerald was desperately insecure about his social standing. He was a financially strapped young writer with enormous social ambition, determined to mingle with the "right" crowd on Long Island.

One of the first people Fitzgerald happened to meet was Tommy Hitchcock, my grandfather's friend, housemate, and protégé. The two men hit it off immediately. Hitchcock invited the Fitzgeralds to parties and helped them put together guest lists for their own soirées. Fitzgerald was immediately enchanted, even obsessed, with Hitchcock. Always lamenting his own lack of athletic talent, he idolized the hard-bodied, Harvard-educated polo star. Like my grandfather, Fitzgerald was fascinated by Hitchcock's offhanded Old Money charm. He also revered Hitchcock's wartime heroism. Although he had enlisted in the army, Fitzgerald never got closer to combat than Camp Sheridan in Montgomery, Alabama. He was disappointed not to have fought in the war that had shaped his generation. As America surged into the glorious 1920s, Fitzgerald's manhood—unlike that of his famous peers Ernest Hemingway and John Dos Passos—remained untested.

When Fitzgerald arrived in Great Neck that fall, he found the social scene so intriguing that the outlines of *The Great Gatsby* took shape in his mind almost immediately. Years later, confirming that source of inspiration, he explained that the first chapter of *Gatsby* was based on "the glamour of the Rumseys and the Hitchcocks." The Rumseys to whom Fitzgerald was referring were Mary Harriman Rumsey and her family. Mary was Averell Harriman's sister. Her husband, Charles Cary Rumsey, had died on September 21, 1922, when the car in which he was a passenger crashed into a stone bridge abutment on the Jericho Turnpike on Long Island. The accident occurred just weeks before the Fitzgeralds moved to Great Neck, and just a few miles from their new home. Under the circumstances, it's hardly surprising that the perils of automobile travel figure so prominently in the novel.

Tommy Hitchcock lodged in Fitzgerald's imagination like a burr. Literary scholars agree that the writer had Hitchcock in his sights when he conceived of Tom Buchanan, the ruthless, blue-blooded polo player married to the beautiful, feckless Daisy. Indeed, according to Hitchcock's son Billy, Fitzgerald

The first edition of *The Great Gatsby*, published by Charles Scribner's Sons in April 1925

The Real Gatsby?

gave Hitchcock a copy of *The Great Gatsby* annotated to mark the many references to him throughout the book. Buchanan appears in the novel's opening chapter fresh off the polo field. Like Hitchcock, Buchanan is an imposing physical specimen. "Not even the effeminate swank of his riding clothes could hide the enormous power of that body," wrote Fitzgerald. "He seemed to fill those glistening boots until he strained the top lacing, and you could see a great pack of muscle shifting when his shoulder moved under his thin coat. It was a body capable of enormous leverage—a cruel body."

Of all the people Fitzgerald met on Long Island, Hitchcock made the most lasting impression on him. Fitzgerald claimed that Hitchcock was his best friend there. When Fitzgerald needed money a few years later, Hitchcock was kind enough to buy one of Zelda's paintings, a modernist nude, to help him out. (Hitchcock's wife, Peggy, was less enchanted with the Fitzgeralds. According to Billy Hitchcock, she dismissed Scott as a "moocher." Billy also said that Peggy did not like Zelda's painting and the couple eventually sold it. He further recalled that his parents paid the dentist's bill when Zelda had her teeth fixed.) Years later, Fitzgerald wrote to his daughter that Hitchcock's heroism and humility had earned him a place in his "pantheon of heroes."

Fitzgerald's decision to base the brutish, bigoted Buchanan on the war hero-athlete Hitchcock reflected his complicated feelings about Hitchcock's wealth and social status. As Fitzgerald supposedly said to Ernest Hemingway, "The rich are different from you and me." Ever aware of his own marginal social standing and lack of money, Fitzgerald perpetually yearned to bridge the insuperable gulf between himself and the rich people of the world. Near the end of his life, he wrote, "That was always my experience—a poor boy in a rich town; a poor boy in a rich boy's school; a poor boy in a rich man's club at Princeton. . . .. I have never been able to forgive the rich for being rich, and it has colored my entire life and works." Perhaps more fully than anyone else in his life, Hitchcock embodied everything that the conflicted writer both worshipped in other people and simultaneously hated them for.

At the time when Fitzgerald was reveling in "the glamour of the Hitchcocks and the Rumseys," Tommy Hitchcock and my grandfather were virtually inseparable. During the week, they lived and worked together in Manhattan. On weekends, they headed out to Long Island for polo and partying. Seeking to establish himself as a North Shore regular, Moore had bought a house in Sands Point, the elite enclave where Mary Rumsey lived. Sands Point loomed large in Fitzgerald's imagination. Visible across Manhasset Bay from Great Neck, it was his inspiration for East Egg, where Daisy Buchanan's lawn "started at the beach and ran toward the front door for a quarter of a mile, jumping over sun-dials and brick walks and burning gardens."

Fitzgerald scholars agree that most of the characters in *Gatsby* are composites of actual people the writer knew or knew about. The identification of Buchanan with Hitchcock is undisputed. In Fitzgerald's 1934 novel, *Tender is the Night*, Hitchcock was also a model for Tommy Barban, the mercenary soldier who made off with the novel's heroine, Nicole Diver.

Fitzgerald was less forthcoming about his inspiration for Gatsby. Literary sleuths have been struggling to solve that mystery for nearly a hundred years. Poring over Fitzgerald's notes and correspondence, scholars have come up with several candidates, including a bootlegger and a Wall Street scammer. These figures bore some resemblance to Gatsby in the most literal sense. They were rich and corrupt, and one reportedly addressed Fitzgerald as "old sport," a phrase often used by Gatsby. The 1920s were awash with the flamboyant decadence of flashy wannabes and overnight millionaires. Moore's lavish lifestyle was hardly unique in this respect. But none of the possible suspects showed the kind of personal flair or zest for living that George Moore did. For Fitzgerald, it was that rare spirit, the unbridled optimism for the future, which defined Gatsby. The literary sleuths didn't know about George Moore.

Several historians and scholars who were familiar with Moore—his outsized passions, his close relationship with Tommy Hitchcock, and his prominence in the New York social circle that embraced Fitzgerald in the early 1920s—have drawn the connection between Moore and Gatsby. Charles R. Morris, a well-known economic historian who wrote extensively about the Great Depression, was familiar with Moore's reputation. He noted that Moore had "entered international society by staging Gatsby-like bacchanals on his Long Island estate and in London" and suggested that Gatsby's "wild parties" may have been modeled after Moore's. Likewise, Nelson Aldrich wrote that Moore "might have sat for the portrait of Jay Gatsby." He described Moore's parties as being "filled with music, lovely girls, handsome men, good food and wine, frequent laughter, and tears." Mark H. Miller, who wrote the definitive history of Rancho San Carlos, agreed. After thoroughly investigating Moore's life and the literary evidence adduced by Fitzgerald scholars, he concluded that Moore was the most likely source for Jay Gatsby. It's tempting to agree that Moore was the missing piece of the Gatsby puzzle.

— CHAPTER 3 —

Wyoming

TALES OF IMMIGRANTS MAKING GOOD are the bedrock of the American story. They confirm our vision of America as a land of opportunity where anyone can succeed if they try hard enough. Growing up, I heard no such inspiring stories about any of my forebears. As far as I knew, I was not descended from pioneers who tamed the wilderness or wily fortune seekers risking their last nickel on some newfangled invention. I assumed my family was respectable and well-to-do as far back as anyone could remember. But that was hardly the case. As I discovered, my grandfather's destiny was forged in that rough, improvisatory world of immigrants and their dreams.

Moore's parents, David and Ruth, were among the 1.5 million people who fled the Irish Potato Famine of the 1840s. They tried their luck twice, and failed both times, at farming in the untamed wilderness of Michigan. With five young children in tow, the Moores moved to Wyoming, Ontario, a small town that had sprung up like a mushroom in the 1860s after oil was discovered nearby in places that came to be called Oil Springs and Petrolia. David found work there as a teamster, hauling crude oil with a team of horses and a wagon from the oilfields to the refineries in Wyoming. The work was dangerous, slow, and difficult. It took an entire day to haul two barrels of oil. Five hundred or more wagons made the journey each day, cutting such a deep trench in the wet clay that the road was called "the canal." Over the next few years David managed to purchase several plots of land in Wyoming and built their log house. Despite their arduous lives, David and Ruth managed to have five more children, the last of whom was my grandfather, George Gordon Moore, born October 1, 1876.

Beyond the Gatsby-like parties, many aspects of my grandfather's unusual pedigree, peregrinations, and personal habits appear like stubborn ghosts in Jay Gatsby's story. Exploring my grandfather's roots, I was reminded of Jay Gatsby's parents, "shiftless and unsuccessful farm people" out in North Dakota. Michigan, like its neighbor to the west, was barely settled when Moore's parents had gone from place to place trying in vain to find enough arable land to farm. Thirty years before Fitzgerald wrote *The Great Gatsby*, North Dakota wasn't even a state. Growing up poor on that crude frontier, Jay Gatsby dreamed constantly of his own "future glory." "The most gross and fantastic conceits haunted him in his bed at night," wrote Fitzgerald. "A universe of ineffable gaudiness spun itself out in his brain while the clock ticked on the washstand and the moon soaked with wet light his tangled clothes upon the floor." Moore also had tremendous dreams and, like Gatsby, he pursued them with dogged determination.

Back in my grandfather's day, the town of Wyoming boasted several hotels, half a dozen grocery stores, two bookstores, various shoemakers and milliners, and dozens of businesses like barrel makers and foundries that were born of the oil industry. But such robust commerce faded away when the oil boom fizzled in the 1920s. When I visited there on a blustery November morning a few years ago, I found a pizza parlor, bank, and hardware store—the usual mainstays of towns left high and dry by the shifting tides of industry—along with more than a few vacant storefronts and a boarded-up hotel. A small sign on a door across from the hotel indicated the local headquarters of the Independent Order of Odd Fellows. A battered yellow sandwich board on the sidewalk advertised the Lions Club's weekly Meat Bingo game. I had never heard of Meat Bingo, but it sounded like a desperate pastime for a town long down on its luck.

"The simple act of building is the surest means of announcing that one has made good," wrote the architecture critic Brendan Gill. Until 1902, Moore's parents had lived in the same log house where Moore was born. As soon as Moore made his first fortune, he built his parents a solid brick house in the newly popular American Foursquare style, a simple, boxy two-story design with each floor divided into four equal spaces. Known as the "Prairie Box," the Foursquare was a radical innovation: an affordable middle-class home design that could be built from a mail-order kit and that featured both electricity and a sink-toilet-bath bathroom. I had no trouble finding the house. Except for the addition of a front entryway, its exterior is unchanged. I felt uneasy about intruding, but I'd come too far not to press further. I screwed up my courage and knocked on the door. After a few moments a woman opened the door a few inches and then a few more, clearly not expecting a visitor so early in the day. She appeared to be around forty and was still in her bathrobe and slippers. I introduced myself and explained who I was and why I was there. She invited me in, eager to hear about my grandfather and the history of the house, of which she knew practically nothing. She apologized for the disheveled condition of the place; she and her husband were in the process of tearing out the cheap hung ceilings and fake wood paneling that previous owners had installed. But the house's architectural details—handsome Queen Anne woodwork, ten-foot ceilings, and transom windows—attested to its original stateliness. It must have seemed like a palace to my great-grandparents. In building the house, my grandfather no doubt wanted to show off his success to his hometown. But he also wanted to give his elderly parents a comfortable berth in which to spend their final years. He was installing them in the middle-class, a place they had worked long and hard to reach.

Moore mausoleum, Wyoming, Ontario

David Moore died in January 1920 and Ruth Moore followed him six weeks later. My grandfather built a grand neoclassical mausoleum for them in the Wyoming cemetery. The granite structure, by far the largest in the cemetery, bears the name "MOORE" prominently carved over the main door. Over the years, the mausoleum has been vandalized.

The Ionic columns have been defaced, the windows shattered. The front door and windows are now boarded up, replaced by heavy wooden panels, painted gray to match the stone exterior. The raw, overcast weather that morning matched the mood of the mausoleum. The sense of desolation reminded me of how unsparing the passage of time can be to our proudest monuments. I thought about Percy Bysshe Shelley's famous sonnet "Ozymandias." A meditation on the transitory nature of self-styled human greatness, the poem describes the fallen statue of a once-powerful king, broken into pieces in the desert sands of "an antique land." My mind is etched with the images of those "vast and trunkless legs of stone" and the "half sunk, shattered visage," along with the pedestal marked with the words

> *"My name is Ozymandias, King of kings:*
> *Look on my works, ye Mighty, and despair!"*

Unlike the ancient statue of Ozymandias, the Moore mausoleum still stands. But its once colorful windows look like blinded eyes, its once proud door like a mouth permanently sealed. As I wandered through the cemetery looking for other Moore descendants, I saw the desecrated structure as the embodiment of my grandfather's long and tumultuous life. The mausoleum was the first of his many noble gestures, a testament to his unwavering optimism for the future.

— CHAPTER 4 —

Gaining Traction

A CARTOON FROM A 1905 compendium called *Our Michigan Friends—As We See 'Em*, shows a fashionably attired young man—hugely oversized—driving a tiny horse and cart down a country road. A metropolis towers in the background. The man's lapel bears a colossal pin in the shape of a trolley, and his pants are made of dollar bills. A fat law book sits beside him, and a bulging bag of money behind him calls out, "I haven't been spent yet." The man pictured is George Moore, just shy of his thirtieth birthday, by which time he was—like Gatsby—a self-made multi-millionaire.

By all accounts, my grandfather was an exceptionally bright and enterprising child. He was said to have had a photographic memory. He spent much of his free time nosing around the refineries and the Wyoming rail station. It was not lost on him that his father labored at a hard and dangerous job for low pay while other men sat at desks getting rich off the oil trade. By age twelve, my grandfather had exhausted the educational offerings of Wyoming. His parents sent him across the border to Port Huron, Michigan, to live with his brother David and attend high school. He graduated two years later.

Although his parents couldn't afford to pay for further education, my grandfather was determined to study law. His intellectual ambition caught the attention of a local attorney named O'Brien J. Atkinson, who took him on as a clerk to read law, a kind of apprenticeship and a common alternative back then to attending law school. My grandfather started at the Port Huron law office shortly before his fifteenth birthday, working his way up from menial tasks such as copying legal documents to drafting bills of sale. On October 17, 1896, he became an American citizen. The following year, at age twenty-one, he was named a partner of the firm of Atkinson, Wolcott & Moore. As a newly minted lawyer, he spent long hours putting together lucrative business deals for clients, hammering out the tedious details of contracts and loan agreements. He soon realized that businessmen, not lawyers, were making the serious money.

My grandfather was not moved to practice law by any personal commitment to justice or public service. For him, law was a ticket to the world of business he had glimpsed in Wyoming and Port Huron. In 1899, when valuable clay deposits were found in nearby St. Clair, Michigan, he joined forces with two new companies to mine and market the clay. In 1900, he and two prominent Port Huron businessmen incorporated the Utility Water Supply Co. for the manufacture of water-pumping equipment. In 1901, he began to buy and sell land in Port Huron. In a pattern that would repeat itself for decades, his dynamic energy and unerring eye for a profitable deal drew a host of wealthy investors.

Central Michigan at the turn of the century was nothing like the inhospitable wilderness Moore's parents had encountered forty years earlier. Industry was expanding, towns were growing into cities. The urban explosion generated an immediate and insatiable demand for rail transportation, both within cities and between them. Horses and carriages were dangerous and unsanitary; they were also incapable of moving large numbers of people and goods through crowded city streets. In Michigan, as elsewhere, independent rail operators obtained franchises from local governments to build trolley lines. The first of these were crude horse-drawn conveyances, but motorized traction quickly developed. By the early 1900s, electric traction systems were replacing horse-powered public transit all across the country.

In 1902, foreseeing a glorious future in the traction business, Moore formed a partnership with a couple of other wealthy businessmen to buy up the hodge-podge of rail lines that ran in and between the growing cities of Kalamazoo, Lansing, and others. By 1905, Moore's partnership owned 193 miles of the most valuable city and interurban rail lines in the state. In 1906, the group consolidated their holdings into the Michigan United Railways, then worth an estimated $5 million, roughly $161 million in today's currency. The financial machinations involved in this consolidation generated a morass of litigation over the next several years. Lawsuits alleging stock-watering, fraud, and other chicanery were widely reported in national newspapers. Despite the accusations, the partnership continued to buy city and interurban lines; by 1907, they controlled central Michigan's urban and interurban systems.

As Moore's businesses thrived, so did his personal life. In 1898, he married a young woman from Port Huron named Elizabeth Murphy. Like Moore, she was the child of Irish immigrants. There is no record of how they met or what sort of courtship or wedding they had. All I know is that Moore was twenty-two and his bride was twenty-one when they married. Moore might have preferred to marry a socialite—that would come in due time—but he settled for a beauty.

The Moores' daughter, Virginia, was born in 1900. Elizabeth Moore traveled frequently to New York, Palm

Beach—where she had a suite at The Breakers—and Europe, attended by her French maid. Virginia sometimes accompanied her. The Port Huron and Detroit newspapers detailed even her most mundane social activities: outings on horseback with lady friends, glee club concerts, visits from her siblings. One report simply noted, "Mrs. George Moore and her daughter are at home." Meanwhile, Moore himself was rarely at home. He was on the road keeping track of his expanding enterprises—including rail and real estate partnerships in Michigan and power companies in Nebraska, Wisconsin, Alabama, Vermont, and Georgia—and hunting down new ventures and sources of capital all over North and South America. By 1905, when the *Our Michigan Friends* caricature was published, Moore was an internationally acclaimed "traction magnate" with a fortune of several million dollars. In 1910, the *Detroit Free Press* wrote that Moore was "probably the youngest man in the universe" to have started from such modest beginnings and to have "grasped and succeeded with gigantic undertakings."

Moore was living the high life. A menu from a banquet he attended in Detroit included "Blue Point Oysters, Green Sea Turtle, Filet of beef larded à la Bayard, Roman Punch, Snow Birds au cresson, asparagus tips, and Cold Fresh Lobster," delicacies that might appear in a dining scene concocted by Merchant and Ivory. It's hard to square such an opulent image with my recollections of the old man dribbling oyster stew down his shirt at Christmas. But as I confront these dueling images, I have the sense I am watching a sentimental old movie in which pages fly off the calendar as the years fly by—in reverse in this case, so that in the space of a few seconds, I have time-traveled nearly a century.

The Moore family moved every couple of years into bigger, more fashionable houses in Port Huron. Around 1907, Moore bought a lavish summer home in nearby St. Clair. He lost no time in putting his own stamp on the enormous Victorian pile. He changed its name from "Belle Reve" to

"Dromore," after the town in Ireland where his mother was born. And although the house was barely eighteen years old, Moore had it remodeled to suit his own taste. He added a curved porch that ran the length of the house and overlooked the picturesque St. Clair River below. He had the entire third floor made into living quarters for his household staff that included two French maids for his wife and daughter, his valet, a butler, and two chauffeurs.

But Moore's most ostentatious piece of remodeling was inspired by his obsession with British nobility. He had visited England several times on business and was enthralled by the country's rich aristocratic heritage. Like so many Gilded Age titans, my grandfather wanted a piece of it for himself. He purchased a roomful of carved wooden paneling from a baronial hall in England and installed it in Dromore House's grand living room. The cost for this patina of nobility was was approximately $4 million in today's currency.

Dromore House was torn down in 1964, irredeemable after many years of neglect. But miraculously, the part of the house that truly embodied my grandfather's spirit, the English paneling, was saved from the wrecking ball. Some of it was eventually installed in the St. Clair Historical Museum. I had seen black and white photographs of the paneling but when I saw it at the museum, tracing with my fingertips its intricately carved faces and cryptic emblems and inhaling its musty scent, I felt I was stepping through the curtain of historical record into the living past. I could see my grandfather choosing the paneling, arranging for its shipping, directing its installation, and showing it off to to admiring neighbors and curiosity seekers.

I recalled the moment when Nick Carraway discovered Gatsby's magnificent "high Gothic" library, "paneled with carved English oak, and probably transported complete from some ruin overseas." Here were two men, Moore and Gatsby, making the same grand but hollow gesture of greatness.

Gaining Traction

Dromore House paneling, now installed at the St. Clair Historical Museum

— CHAPTER 5 —

The Racing Life

ALTHOUGH MY GRANDFATHER visited our family only once a year, he was a regular presence in our lives through the telegrams he sent regarding news of my parents' horses. A typical message would read, "Great win with Trojan's Broom. I hope you won't risk that filly in another claiming race." Or, "Congratulations on buying the Knightly Manner colt. He'll stay the distance."

Horseracing was the bedrock of my family's life. While most of my friends' parents subscribed to *Life* magazine and *Newsweek,* our house was littered with horse sales catalogs, stallion registers, and magazines like *Blood Horse* and the *Thoroughbred Record.* On the infrequent occasions when my parents included my siblings and me in their travels, we spent much of our time sulking in the car while my father scouted out newsstands in seedy neighborhoods in search of the *New York Morning Telegraph.* This newspaper (now the *Daily Racing Form*) was a daily entertainment broadsheet that contained detailed information about the day's races and the horses' past performances. It was invaluable to horse people and handicappers. The *Telegraph* was my father's bible. After gleaning the specifics he sought from its pages, he would find a pay phone and make long-distance calls, presumably to his trainer and his bookie. We might make it to the beach, or the riding stable, or the hiking trail, by early afternoon.

Most Saturday mornings our parents took us to the racetrack to watch the horses work out. Jennie and I were horse-crazy and loved these junkets. We nervously let the horses nuzzle carrots from our outstretched hands. My parents' trainer, a gruff old Virginian named Aubrey Fishback, would occasionally let us ride his lead pony, Trigger, a patient palomino with long yellow teeth. My brother Gordon was less enthusiastic about these activities, but the experience must have imprinted his imagination at a deeper level, because he ended up working on the New York racing circuit for many years.

After morning workouts, we would go to the track kitchen for breakfast. This place, too drab to be called a restaurant, always smelled of tobacco smoke, greasy eggs and bacon, coffee, and piney liniment. In the summer, strips of yellow flypaper speckled black with flies dangled from the ceiling over the cash register and just inside the screen door. The track kitchen attracted a rich gumbo of humanity. Jennie and I were particularly fascinated by the jockeys and exercise riders. Some were young and pimply-faced, not much older than us. Others were grizzled and gimpy from too many falls from fractious, barely saddle-broke horses. (This was the 1960s, years before anyone wore protective helmets or Kevlar vests.) While we ate pancakes and sausages, my parents chatted with trainers wearing tweed caps and corduroy. Every manner of horse person, from veterinarians and blacksmiths in their coveralls to hot-walkers and gamblers, would slouch over the pockmarked linoleum counter drinking coffee, smoking cigarettes, and handicapping the day's races.

The horse races took place in the afternoon. Like everyone else in the racing world, my parents were superstitious. On racing days, there would be frantic searches for my father's "lucky" tie or the dress my mother had worn the last time the horse had won. My father always made sure they had their binoculars and a Scotch cooler filled with the rum punch that he and my mother drank on the way to the track. Their horses lost far more races than they won, but the wins were glorious. We would rush down to the winner's circle to be photographed with the horse and jockey. The walls of our guest bathroom were painted in our racing colors, lavender and red (chosen by my mother from a Degas racing scene) and lined with photographs from the winner's circle showing Gordon, reluctantly wearing a coat and tie, and Jennie and me in our matching Villager-brand shirtwaist dresses and penny loafers. Sometimes my parents celebrated the victory by stopping for dinner at some smoky steakhouse on the way home. Fellow racetrackers would come by to congratulate them and sometimes even send a bottle of champagne to our table.

The car rides home after the races seemed much longer when the horse had run poorly. My father would smoke a cigar and grumble while my mother, who knew far more about horses than my father, offered explanations for the disappointing performance. Perhaps the jockey didn't send the horse to the front soon enough. Or perhaps there was a training problem. Was the horse fit enough for the distance? Did it need more experience breaking from the starting gate? Eventually she would raise my father's spirits by reading aloud about upcoming races in the track's "condition book." In the racing world, there was always another day.

When I was ten, my parents bought a small farm in the horse-centric town of Middleburg, Virginia. Even before the barn was finished, they acquired a couple of Thoroughbred broodmares and a few mixed-breed horses that we rode around the countryside. Over the years my parents bought, bred, and sold many racehorses. Their occasional success was entirely due to my mother's knowledge of horses and her talent for picking good bloodlines. Unfortunately, she yielded too often to my father's uninformed and impetuous decisions—in large part, I suspect, for the future pleasure of scolding him for not listening to her. When something went badly—if they sold a broodmare for cheap that went on to produce stakes winners, or they lost a promising young horse in a claiming race—she would shake her head and say, "It was *Duffy's* idea," referring to my father by his nickname. And it usually was.

As I learned later, my mother could well have inherited her uncanny savvy about horses and pedigrees from her father. I knew that my grandfather was a racing fan, not only from his telegrams but also because of how carefully he clocked morning workouts at the racetrack when he came east. But I did not know that he had been personally involved in horseracing. Back in the early 1900s, he was one of America's most prominent breeders and owners of Standardbred trotting horses. Given that horse racing dominated our family's life, it's puzzling why my grandfather's remarkable success was never mentioned. In my parents' rarified world of Thoroughbred racing, Standardbred racing was considered low class. Was my mother embarrassed to talk about it? Could she have forgotten tales from her father's past that had taken place in what seemed to her an earlier lifetime? I doubt she would have forgotten stories about record-breaking horses. Had her father caused her so much pain that she simply couldn't bear to talk about his life? Possibly. Or perhaps my mother never knew much about her father's early experience with horseracing. There was a lot she didn't know about the life he led before she was born.

As a youngster, Moore had developed a deep appreciation and knowledge of horses. It could hardly have been otherwise. His family's livelihood depended on maintaining a solid team of draft horses to work in the oilfields. He knew that teaming, as it was known, was dangerous work. A horse's soundness, strength, and mental acuity were essential. A lame step or missed signal could be costly if not fatal. Good horsemanship and an eye for equine conformation and intelligence were instilled in him early on.

In the 1890s and early 1900s, Standardbred harness racing was one of the most popular entertainments for America's elite. Unlike Thoroughbred racing, a sport in which horses are ridden by jockeys around a track galloping full tilt, Standardbreds trot at lightning speed pulling their drivers in lightweight carts called sulkies. My grandfather had grown up mucking out stables and poulticing horses' hooves. Harness racing was his holy grail. In 1902, the same year that Moore built his parents a house, he bought his first racehorse, a Standardbred named Marshall. Although the horse never won a race for my grandfather, his lackluster record was beside the point. With his purchase of Marshall, Moore crossed the great divide between people who kept horses for work and those who kept them for sport.

In 1907, Moore bought a 650-acre horse farm across the road from his summer home in St. Clair and named it Dromore Stock Farm. He was determined to build the best breeding and racing operation in the country. With his photographic memory, he quickly mastered the constellations of Standardbred bloodlines. He scoured the country for top-quality breeding stock, sparing no expense. The year after he founded Dromore Stock Farm, one sportswriter commented, "If this establishment fails to send out race winners the fault won't be in the quality of the material used for breeding purposes."

Moore poured even more money into the racing side of his business. He hired the country's best trainers and built a weatherproof enclosure around the half-mile track at Dromore—an unheard-of extravagance in those days—so that horses could train there year-round. My grandfather's investments paid off. In 1910, his stable included Justice Brooke, a two-year-old homebred colt that my grandfather named after his good friend Flavius Lionel Brooke, a member of the Michigan Supreme Court. That summer Justice Brooke won the Kentucky Futurity, the most prestigious race for two-year-old Standardbreds in the country. In winning what was roughly the equivalent of the Kentucky Derby, Justice Brooke set a record for his age group.

My grandfather spent every spare minute following his horses. "Nothing gives me as much pleasure as to see my horses," he told a reporter in 1910. "It costs So-and-So a lot of money to keep up his steam yacht. I have just as much right to indulge my particular fancy." Over the next few years, Dromore continued to produce a steady stream of champions. Wins and impressive morning workouts garnered headlines. On one occasion when Dromore horses were shipped by train to Kentucky, the *Detroit Free Press* reported that they "are traveling in a special car in which they will have every comfort that is possible . . . as equine kings and queens and heirs apparent have the right to expect."

By 1919, harness racing had begun to lose its glamour. My grandfather auctioned off his legendary band of broodmares. He had already turned his attention to other sporting endeavors, including hunting and polo. But he never fully left harness racing behind; his Dromore credentials would continue to surface occasionally, serendipitously altering the course of his life.

— CHAPTER 6 —

"I Discovered England"

Perhaps Jay Gatsby's most memorable idiosyncrasy was his habit of peppering his conversation with British phrases like "old sport." To fill out Gatsby's mysterious past, Fitzgerald had given him a stint at Oxford after the war, which accounted for his Old World affectation. My grandfather, too, had spent time in England before and during the war; he proudly bore the traces of his years abroad when he returned from England and settled in New York.

When my grandfather died in 1971, my mother flew out to Los Angeles for a couple of days to clean out his apartment and tie up the loose ends of his final years. If there were any interesting papers or other mementos, she did not save them. It's a minor miracle that years later, after my father's death in 2009, I stumbled on a cache of papers that provided information about my grandfather's sojourn in England, which I might never have known about. These papers had been tucked into a tattered old legal file that was destined for the town dump.

My father had practiced law at a large Washington, D.C., firm. As a specialist in banking and pharmaceutical regulations, he must have paid attention to details at work. At home, however, he was Mr. Magoo. After my mother died of emphysema in 2005, things at the farm began to unravel. My father wasn't sure which broodmares were in foal or whether he had paid his housekeeper or had his Coumadin levels checked. My siblings and I did our best to keep the last years of his life in order, but it was hard going.

In his will, my father named me executor of his estate. Shortly after his death we put the family farm up for sale. It was a sad decision, but none of us could afford to keep it going. In the months following my father's death we spent many hours sorting through my parents' belongings, which were stashed in drawers and closets all over the house. We shook our heads in disbelief when we discovered empty vodka bottles my mother had hidden in old riding boots. She had been even sneakier than we had known. She had often written random thoughts about books she was reading, or conversations she'd had, on stray pieces of paper, including refund and dividend checks, usually for amounts less than $100. Coming across these, I recalled her brilliant, quirky mind and pondered the irony of her pathological frugality. She had discovered the utility of duct tape for repairing clothing years before anyone else had heard of it. The kitchen cabinets held cans of Campbell's beef consommé that were older than I was.

In the end, there wasn't much in the house worth keeping. A devastating fire in 1989 had all but destroyed the house and most of my parents' furniture, rugs, photograph albums, and personal papers. But I felt compelled to cast an eye over everything that remained. I didn't want to throw out anything that might have legal or financial implications for the estate. It was slow work. I took to the dump many carloads of catalogs and old magazines whose covers were speckled white with spider droppings, along with expired car registrations and instruction manuals for appliances long deceased.

Near the end of my due diligence, when I was glassy-eyed and hurrying to finish up, I came across two faded blue-clad binders from my father's law office. These binders contained my father's correspondence with my grandfather, who had consulted him on business matters from the 1960s till his death in 1971. I set them apart from the boxes and bags destined for the landfill and took them home to Massachusetts, along with boxes of china that had belonged to my grandmother and some books that had been salvaged from the fire—Will James's *Smoky the Cow Horse*, volumes of poetry by Robinson Jeffers, who had been a close friend of my mother's family, and Federico Tesio's *Breeding the Racehorse*, a text my parents cherished.

My chance discovery of my grandfather's late correspondence with my father once again stoked my desire to explore my mother's family history. I didn't hold out much hope of finding anything of interest in the files. But research is like betting on the races: one is always hopeful, no matter how slight the odds of success. The files contained mostly papers related to dodgy investment schemes my grandfather had tried to cobble together in his waning years. Interspersed with his drafts of contracts and payout schedules were fuzzy carbon copies of my father's letters chronicling our family's modest triumphs. News of winning racehorses got equal billing with the children's school reports ("Heronswood won a good allowance race at Pimlico. Gordon doing very well at St. Albans School.").

Among these business proposals and prosaic accounts of our family's life, I found a twelve-page typewritten document from around 1960 titled:

The Great War
George Gordon Moore
His story
The outline planned

"I Discovered England"

This brief narrative revealed a chapter in my grandfather's life so extraordinary I assumed it was heavily exaggerated if not completely fabricated. I scoured World War I histories and memoirs and contemporaneous newspaper accounts to see if there was any truth to his story. And to my astonishment, his name turned up in all the places where I might have guessed it would, and in other places too.

My grandfather's memoir began, "I discovered England in 1908, at the time I was building the Michigan United Railways." As he explained, he set his sights on England because he needed capital to fund his growing railroad empire. The Knickerbocker Trust Company, one of the biggest banks in the United States, had just undergone a credit crisis that spread throughout the financial system, bringing about the Panic of 1907. Meanwhile, across the Atlantic, the British had amassed more capital than they knew what to do with. They were eager for investment opportunities in the endlessly bountiful New World. But there was more driving him across the Atlantic than the Panic of 1907 and the resulting credit crunch. Moore's dubious business practices had landed him in hot water with at least one disgruntled debtor in a dispute that would end up in litigation. England would provide a clean slate for him.

Apart from his legal problems and need for new capital, Moore's rapacious social ambition also drew him to London. In America, he belonged to all the right clubs; he rode in private railroad cars; he stayed in the best hotels and ate at the finest restaurants. At this point he set his sights on more elite territory. With its deep-pocketed aristocrats, what venue could have been more alluring than London? England would be his next great adventure. And so he proclaimed, "I discovered England in 1908"—the words of a would-be conqueror.

By 1908, Moore was an internationally acclaimed wizard of American industry. He had no trouble persuading British investors to put their money into his expanding network of railroads and power companies in the United States. He orchestrated these investments by selling bonds in Michigan United Railways to the Investment Registry, Ltd., a prestigious financial institution that had been organized in London in 1880 by a committee of British army and naval officers. Its aim was to provide investors—military brass and aristocrats—with a diversified portfolio of stocks and bonds, mainly in the developing economies of North and South America. Over the next few years Moore channeled huge amounts of British cash from the coffers of the Investment Registry into various American promotions. By June of 1912, he owned a controlling interest in the Registry. "For the first time in my life," he wrote, "I was free of debt, and had several million dollars on hand, one year before there were any income taxes."

As I sorted through the shards of my grandfather's early life, I was amazed by the breadth of his undertakings. Back in the early 1900s, when people traveled by train and boat and communicated primarily by mail and telegraph, it seems inconceivable that one man, no matter how wealthy, could have simultaneously managed so many far-flung projects. He owned a multimillion-dollar railroad system in the Midwest; he bought and sold power companies in several states; he bred championship racehorses and sporting dogs at his farm in Michigan. But his life was of a piece with his times, an era of expansive optimism when it was possible to reinvent oneself repeatedly, like a stage actor playing multiple roles in a single drama. Within a year of "discovering England," he had parlayed a North Carolina timber investment into an exotic hunting preserve in the wilds of the Smoky Mountains.

— CHAPTER 7 —

Hunting Pigs in Paradise

A T THE TURN OF THE TWENTIETH CENTURY, logging was king in the mountains of western North Carolina. The advent of railroads and steam-powered machines, coupled with a huge demand for lumber on the East Coast and in Europe, had triggered a boom in the timber industry. Roads were few, and a network of single-gauge railroads was built to haul timber from newly accessible virgin forests to mills back east. In 1909, Moore purchased 100,000 acres of prime timberland in Graham County, near the town of Robbinsville, on behalf of a British syndicate called Whiting Manufacturing. Back then, it wasn't unusual to see businessmen like Moore passing through to negotiate deals with local logging outfits and railroad companies. Most of these men spent just enough time in the outback to see to their timber interests before fleeing back to civilization.

Moore wasn't in such a hurry to leave. As his broker's fee—what he called his "perquisite"—he claimed a long-term lease on 1,600 acres of land at the top of Hooper Bald, one of the tallest points in the Smokies, at 5,429 feet. Moore had big plans. His aim was to create a hunting preserve in the tradition of Gilded Age getaways, places where America's aristocrats—the Roosevelts, the Whitneys, the Vanderbilts—traveled to fish, hunt, and "rough it" with friends and family. For a socially ambitious millionaire, a private game preserve was the quintessential emblem of privilege. Moore had the money and determination to make it happen.

I learned about this outlandish scheme several years ago when a distant cousin sent me a copy of a four-page, single-spaced letter written by my grandfather in 1963. The letter described the series of events that had put him in possession of a hunting lodge in the Smoky Mountains and a herd of ferocious wild boar. The letter was addressed to Stuyvesant Fish. "Stuyvie," as he was known, was my mother's step-brother, the son of my grandmother's fourth and final husband, Sidney Fish, who owned the Palo Corona Ranch in Carmel. The letter began, "Dear Stuyvie: You would like to know where the wild boar originated that I turned loose on Rancho San Carlos. It involves two names that you probably never heard of: The Investment Registry, 2 Waterloo Place, London, England, and Walter Winans, an American sportsman with a country place in Kent County, England. To answer your questions without these names would be like Hamlet without the Prince of Denmark." My grandfather's tales—including the details of this one, which I subsequently learned—were as improbable as Jay Gatsby's claims about living "like a young rajah in all the capitals of Europe—Paris, Venice, Rome—collecting jewels, chiefly rubies, hunting big game. . . ." I wondered if any part of them could be true.

I made a phone call to the chamber of commerce in Robbinsville and was put in touch with a woman named Carolyn Stewart, the register of deeds for Graham County. Much to my surprise, she knew all about George Gordon Moore. As she made clear, he is a legendary figure in that part of the world. She told me that nothing remains of his fabled hunting lodge except stories that the locals still tell, some of which have been recorded in histories of the area. She encouraged me to visit, assuring me that she would put me in touch with people whose forebears had worked for my grandfather.

Hunting Pigs in Paradise

On Columbus Day weekend in 2014, I flew into Asheville, North Carolina, at the eastern edge of the Smokies. In preparation for my trip to Robbinsville, I stopped by Mast General Store—Asheville's version of L.L. Bean—to buy a map of hiking trails and natural features in the Robbinsville area. I found the map I was looking for, and when I saw the name "Hooper Bald" in tiny print next to a spot where the contour lines bunched, my pulse quickened. Hooper Bald suddenly became a real place in my mind, not just an odd name in an old typewritten letter. I asked the young cashier if he had any advice about traveling to Robbinsville. Chuckling quietly, he responded, "Yes, don't go there." I couldn't tell if he was kidding. But when he told me it was in the poorest county in North Carolina, with raging unemployment and a ruinous methamphetamine problem, I knew he was serious. I asked if there was anything I should be aware of.

"Not the wildlife" was his reply.

I left Asheville and headed west for Robbinsville, a drive of about two hours. With every mile my sense of remoteness grew. The spaces between towns along the highway increased. Roadside businesses looked sadder and more dilapidated. At the sign for Robbinsville, I turned onto a road that looped through the remains of the original town. Snider's Department Store, an old movie theater, and a few other storefronts hinted at former good fortune. Back on the highway, I found the town's commercial district, if you could call it that—a stretch of highway with a Dollar General and a handful of other local businesses. A sign on the roadside announced that Robbinsville's second annual Wild Meat Festival was taking place that same afternoon. I found the gathering in a gravel parking lot across from a grocery store. I pulled over and parked in a row of mud-spattered pickup trucks, some with hound crates in the back. Dark clouds hung over the mountains, casting them in black shadow. The October air was cool with drizzle that threatened to become rain.

Truckloads of mountain people were arriving, and the atmosphere in the parking lot began to shift into party mode. Sullen-faced teenaged girls with rainbow streaks in their tight, high ponytails slouched around the edges of the parking lot, flirting lazily with young men wearing camo-colored clothes and tractor caps. Pasty-faced young mothers smoked cigarettes and watched over pudgy toddlers playing in the wet gravel. Rowdy rockabilly blasted from loudspeakers. Men were setting up a bandstand and laying down a temporary plywood dance floor. An ominous rumble signaled the arrival of a dozen or so motorcycles whose engines sputtered in the parking lot. The riders, clad in black leather jackets and jeans, looked to be middle-aged, with greasy hair and tanned, leathery skin. No one looked healthy. Even the teenagers had crooked, tobacco-stained teeth.

I went over to a makeshift food station where a line of people waited to be served. Wild boar, stewed or barbecued, was the main attraction. The rancid, sweet smell of damp wood smoke mingled with the odor of gamey, oily meat. A dozen or so sun-wizened women, hair tied back with kerchiefs, dished out chunks of boar along with bear meat casserole and breaded fried trout. Tubs of coleslaw and macaroni salad rounded out the meal. I had no appetite, but I reluctantly accepted a spoonful of each offering on my flimsy paper plate. I pulled out my wallet to pay but a young woman told me the meal was free. "Against the law to sell wild-caught meat," she explained.

I sat down at an empty picnic table. As I contemplated the brown gobbets of meat congealing on the plate, I was overcome by the shameful childhood memory of facing down a plate of calves' liver and waiting in disgrace until my parents gave up and dismissed me from the table. I speared a small cube of stewed boar with my plastic fork. Gamey did not begin to describe the taste and texture of the meat. I chewed just long enough to feel confident I could swallow it without choking. I chased it with a greasy wafer of trout. The bear casserole seemed a bridge too far, but I ventured on. It tasted just like what I imagined bear would taste like. Yuck. An impromptu to-do list popped into my mind: sample wild meat dinner. Check.

At the back of the parking lot were several booths promoting various local interests. I approached a heavily tattooed young man representing the Robbinsville Shooting Company and explained that I had come to Robbinsville to find out what I could about my grandfather and his hunting lodge. I mentioned the exotic animals he'd brought into the neighborhood.

"It was your grandpa who brought in the Rooshians?" he asked.

"Rooshians?" I repeated, not understanding what he meant.

"The boar," he explained. "We call 'em Rooshians because they came from Russia."

"Yup, that was my grandpa," I answered. I felt uneasy applying that endearing moniker to the old man I had always addressed as "Grandfather."

He called a friend over to the table, announcing "Hey, this lady's grandpa brought the Rooshians to Hupper Bald."

Looking me up and down, the friend said, "Well, ma'am, you're not gonna be so pop'lar 'round here if you tell folks it was your grandpa who brought in the Rooshians." He told me about how the boar dug up farm fields, ruining entire crops of potatoes or corn or anything else a farmer might plant. "Their tusks are so sharp they could root up concrete if they put their mind to it," he said.

The Shooting Company man said, "Boar huntin' season opens Monday." His squinty blue eyes lit up. "Lookin' forward to it."

I wished them good luck with their hunting and made my way over to the Joyce Kilmer Forest booth, staffed by a gray-haired man in a khaki forest ranger uniform. Again I explained my mission. Echoing the clerk in Mast General Store, he lamented the sorry state of the local economy. "Trouble is, it's a dry county," he said. In other words, no nightlife, no tourism, no money. My heart sank at the prospect of tee-totaling for the next three days, especially on a diet of bear casserole. I told him I had booked a room at Snowbird Mountain Lodge, the only accommodation in the area I could find that didn't cater specifically to motorcyclists. I asked hopefully if they served alcohol. "Yes, they do," he said. He explained that hotels in Graham County that qualified as "resorts" could carry liquor licenses, and that to qualify as a resort, a hotel needed to have either a tennis court or a golf course. "So when the new innkeeper took over the lodge a few years ago," he said, "damned if he didn't build a tennis court. Helluva lot easier than putting in a golf course."

I asked about moonshine. "It's not illegal to *make* moonshine," he told me. "It's just illegal to *sell* it." He said that people who wanted more than an alcohol buzz turned to another local cottage industry: methamphetamine. That afternoon I'd seen faces marked by vacant eyes and missing teeth, tell-tale signs of the scourge that was ravaging Appalachia and the rest of the country. Suddenly I was at ground zero of the hideous nationwide epidemic that, up till that moment, had been nothing more to me than a grim news story.

As I made my way up the steep, twisting road to Snowbird Mountain Lodge, I began to worry about my lodgings. I imagined a gloomy bar with a few bedrooms upstairs that looked out over a crabgrass-ridden rectangle of concrete bisected by a sagging net: a Robbinsville-style resort. Arriving at the end of the lodge's long, winding driveway, I was relieved to see a handsome timber and stone building nestled into the mountainside. The lodge, as I learned later, had been built in 1941 as a destination for upscale tourists from Chicago.

I carried my bags up the broad stone staircase to the patio and looked out at the view. Mountains like folds of green velvet, garnished with wisps of fog, surrounded me in every direction. At an altitude of 3,000 feet, the air felt bracingly fresh. I took a deep breath, hoping to expel the smell of damp smoke and greasy meat that still lingered in my nostrils.

— CHAPTER 8 —

Cowboy and Cotton

THE NEXT DAY, SUNDAY, Carolyn Stewart's brother-in-law, a local Baptist pastor named Daniel Stewart, came to pick me up in his shiny black pickup truck. He had agreed to take me to Hooper Bald, where he had a cabin a stone's throw from where my grandfather's hunting lodge had once stood. Well over six feet tall, he introduced himself with a knuckle-crunching handshake. His face, with its strong, square features, fiery blue eyes, mane of silver hair and carefully trimmed beard, looked straight out of a Civil War daguerreotype. He had come directly from preaching and was still wearing his ecclesiastical regalia: a Western-style black suit, black leather cowboy boots, and a bold red-and-white tie fixed with a horsehead tie tack. As I climbed into the truck, I spied his black cowboy hat in the back seat.

We headed west on the Cherohala Highway, which had opened in 1969, replacing a winding, rutted dirt road that had made automobile travel rough going. He sped in and out of fog banks hugging hairpin turns on the edge of the mountain, ascending 2,500 feet in the space of twelve miles. As we drove, Stewart held forth in his booming preacher's voice about the poverty and unemployment in Graham County. "Used to be you could make a living cutting timber. Then the government took over all the land," he said—I guessed that he was referring to the creation of the Smoky Mountain

National Park in 1934—"so you can't do that anymore. That's not right. God told Adam and Eve to tend the garden." He segued into a tirade against methamphetamine. "So many beautiful young girls with their teeth rotted out and their lives ruined," he said. "And they'll do *anything* to get it." He paused to let this grim scenario sink in.

Stewart turned onto an unpaved road and unlocked a metal gate. A hundred years ago, this had been the driveway to my grandfather's lodge. When my grandfather had first arrived at Hooper Bald, it was accessible only by foot or on horseback. To build his compound, he hired a group of locals including Stewart's father and a young man named Garland McGuire, known as "Cotton" because of his nearly white hair. Their first job was to build a twenty-mile road so that ox-drawn wagons could bring in supplies from Andrews, the nearest town. As quickly as building materials could be delivered, they began constructing the hunting lodge (the "Big House") and a caretaker's cabin for McGuire (the "Little House").

Moore's hunting lodge on Hooper Bald, c. 1918

The caretaker's cabin, c. 1918

Cotton McGuire, c. 1918

When construction was finally finished on the lodge, Moore began to entertain his friends there. Cotton McGuire would pick up Moore and his friends at the train station in Murphy and bring them to the lodge, a trip of three hours in a mule-drawn wagon. Moore's trunks were filled with hunting attire, liquor, and fancy food, all part of his vainglorious attempt to civilize the wilderness. It was more than a mile from the gate to the top of Hooper Bald. Hints of yellow and orange tinged the tulip poplars, chestnuts, and oaks that flanked the road. I thought of my grandfather in his stylish British tweeds, admiring the landscape from a seat on McGuire's lurching wagon. Years later, in his letter to Stuyvie Fish, he wrote, "nowhere have I ever seen anything so beautiful as this wild section of the Great Smokies—rhododendrons 40 feet high; the widest variety of foliage imaginable and a view of three states from Hooper Bald Mountain, the highest peak in the center of it."

Stewart continued talking as we drove. "One time when Cotton brought your grandpa up here," he said, "your grandpa went inside to make a phone call. Next thing Cotton knew, your grandpa told him he needed to go back to New York immediately. So the next morning they drove the three hours back to Murphy." I sensed disapproval in his voice, scorn for wealthy, careless outsiders like my grandfather. And me, perhaps. I asked Stewart what people had thought of my grandfather back then. "They were amazed by him," he answered. "No one had ever known anyone like him." I got the sense that in this remote part of the world, Moore had seemed a magic maker.

We parked at the top of the bald, an open, grassy plateau, and got out of the truck. The preacher led me to a place near the center, where the Big House had stood looking out over the mountains. Nothing remains of that fanciful construction except for several heaps of large stones that had made up the foundation. It was another Ozymandias moment for me.

Although the Smoky Mountains were crawling with wild game when Moore arrived—black bear, deer, game birds galore—he worried that the local fauna would not provide enough sporting challenge. He spent the next few years collecting a virtual Noah's Ark of big-game animals—Russian wild boars, brown bears from Germany, buffalo, mule deer, and elk from Colorado. The menagerie arrived by train in the spring of 1911 at the depot in the small town of Murphy. People came from miles around to witness the spectacle. The bellows and rumbles emanating from the train cars were deafening, the stench overpowering. A crew of men wrangled the captive beasts onto wagons—ten men were needed to handle a single buffalo—and headed north. The trip to Hooper Bald over a crude logging road took three days.

As my grandfather had explained in his letter to Stuyvie Fish, the boars had their own peculiar origin story. In the fall of 1910, Moore met an extraordinarily rich American expatriate named Walter Winans, an ardent follower of American harness racing who knew of Moore's record-breaking winner, Justice Brooke. Winans's other passion, Moore soon learned, was boar hunting, a sport that was undergoing a robust revival in Europe, particularly among royalty. Winans had a private hunting preserve in Belgium and agreed to take Moore on a boar hunt there. Thrilled by the risk of danger posed by angry wild boars, Moore decided to add them to his collection of game animals. He asked Winans's dealer for a price on three males and nine females, "the biggest and the toughest he could find anywhere." Moore was soon the owner of twelve boars from the Ural Mountains of Russia.

To contain the boars, my grandfather had directed Cotton McGuire and his crew to build a 500-acre enclosure fenced with thick chestnut rails. For the other animals, the men surrounded a 1,000-acre lot with a ten-foot tall barbed-wire fence, an operation that required twenty-five tons of double-stranded barbed wire. The alien beasts caused nothing but trouble. The bears had no difficulty climbing out of their wire enclosure. Having lived in captivity as zoo animals, they were all too comfortable with humans and frequently appeared at the hunting lodge demanding to be fed. One night, Moore arrived at Hooper Bald to find one of his guests, a young Englishman, with his arm and leg bandaged from wounds he suffered trying to oust a bear from his room. With his usual insouciance, my grandfather claimed to have found the bears' antics "amusing."

More vexing than the bears were the boars. Although one of the sows died on the journey to Hooper Bald, the others felt right at home in their new habitat and multiplied rapidly. Like the bears, the boars easily escaped their split-rail enclosure. One evening a boar charged one of Moore's hunting guides. "I climbed a rock high enough to miss him," he told Moore later, "but he stayed there all night watching me until noon the next day."

Moore soon discovered that local hounds were not up to the challenge of boar hunting and were frequently gored by their ferocious tusked quarry. By crossing an Irish wolfhound—a breed described as "fast enough to catch a wolf and strong enough to kill it"—with a Great Dane, Moore produced a hound that, as he put it, "could creditably hold its own." Moore's prey did not disappoint. Despite their short legs and heavy bodies—a mature wild boar weighs between 200 and 300 pounds—boars are fast, athletic, and aggressive. "Wild boar always have the initiative," Moore told Stuyvie. "You can never tell whether they'll run away from you or run at you, all the action any hunter wants." He and his friends would go out in the fall with one of his hired hunters and a pack of hounds. One of Moore's guests was Stuyvie's uncle Hamilton Fish III. He was determined to kill a boar so that he could take its head back to the Porcellian Club at Harvard, where he was a member. Unfortunately, when he took a shot at a boar, he missed his target and hit and killed the favorite coonhound of Moore's chief hunter, Devereaux Birchfield. "In those days human life was a cheap commodity in the Great Smokies," wrote Moore. "A good coonhound was slightly more valued than a child. Devereaux Birchfield had already killed three men for less important causes than the death of his coonhound. I suddenly found that I had urgent business elsewhere and early the next morning our entire party returned to New York."

When I returned to Snowbird Mountain Lodge that evening after visiting Hooper Bald, I had a chat with the innkeeper. Like the other locals I'd encountered, Robert Rankin knew all about my grandfather's hunting lodge. When I mentioned that I had spent the afternoon with Daniel Stewart, he smiled and said, "So you met the Cowboy Preacher." He told me that he had gotten along well with Stewart until he built the tennis court that secured a liquor license for the inn. "When I got the liquor license," Rankin recalled, "he came storming in here and called me the spawn of Satan."

The next morning, I called on Cotton McGuire's daughter, Helen Louise Wilkey, who was still living in Robbinsville with her husband, Blake. Helen Louise was eager to tell me about her childhood on Hooper Bald. In 1939, when she was seven years old, the Little House had burned down and her family moved into the Big House. She showed me photographs of the Big House, constructed of huge chestnut beams topped by a pitched shingle roof that extended far out over the sides. The living room and kitchen stood at either end. In between were the dining room, two bathrooms, and ten bedrooms, five on each side opening onto a central hallway. When Helen Louise and her family moved in after the fire, the house had stood empty for a decade or more. It was still outfitted with

Moore's handsome hickory furniture, and its rough-hewn walls were hung with heads of bear, boar, and buffalo. Local curiosity seekers made their way up the Bald just to see the indoor bathrooms with their modern toilets and hot-water bathtubs. "Even after we moved in, we all used outhouses and took baths in washtubs," she said. "No one had ever seen a commode or a real bathtub." In addition to indoor bathrooms, my grandfather had installed a telephone—another first for Graham County—a feat that required stringing telephone wires through the mountains from a town called Marble, more than twenty miles to the southeast. Not content with kerosene lanterns, Moore also installed state-of-the-art Delco electric lights, a system powered by a small internal combustion generator that had recently been invented.

Helen Louise remembered life in the Big House vividly. "It was impossible to keep it warm in the winter," she said. The main source of heat was the living room fireplace, which was big enough to hold the five-foot logs that were dragged by mule teams to the lodge. Helen Louise's mother did all the cooking in the fireplace. The family's groceries came once a week on the train from Robbinsville. "Sometimes we only had oatmeal and rice to eat," she said. "Breakfast was rice and gravy." She had heard her parents talk about the food Moore would bring to Hooper Bald—oranges, candies, French champagne, delicacies that never graced her family's table.

As eye-opening as my Smoky Mountain sojourn had been, the most remarkable moment of all came during my visit with Helen Louise. Out of the blue she announced that she had in her possession a letter that my mother had written many years earlier to a woman named Betty Kirby. I knew that Betty Kirby and her husband had been good friends of my parents, though a generation older. They had known my grandfather in Carmel. According to Helen Louise, the Kirbys, inspired by my grandfather's tales of Hooper Bald, had built their own cabin in Robbinsville. They hired Blake Wilkey to construct it and retained him afterwards to look after the property during their long absences. Blake, who died in 2019, told me that he had enjoyed the Kirbys' visits and had been amused by the many vermouth and gin bottles he had hauled away in the trash.

Helen Louise explained that when the Kirbys had first arrived in Robbinsville, they told her that they had known the infamous George Moore of Hooper Bald. They also mentioned that they were still close friends with Moore's daughter, my mother. For some reason, probably as proof of their connection to Moore, Betty had given this letter of my mother's to Helen Louise. She pulled out the letter and handed it to me. The sight of my mother's familiar handwriting on her pale blue Crane's stationery made me feel that her spirit had entered the room. I could almost smell her Chanel No. 5 emanating from the paper. I scanned the letter. "Dear Betty," it began. "We were sorry to miss you in Florida this past spring. Duffy and I had had a hard year—work—child illness, etc. and never knew when we could take off." I checked the date: June 12, 1972. What was my mother referring to? To me, illness meant cancer, meningitis. None of us had ever been seriously ill. What had happened back then?

It took me a few seconds to do the math. This had been my family's annus horribilis, starting on July 4th weekend 1971, when Jennie had gone to a rally for marijuana legalization on the Mall in Washington, D.C. Two weeks shy of her eighteenth birthday, she had recently graduated from the Woodstock Country School, a now-defunct boarding school in Vermont that was fueled mostly by drugs and alcohol. Many of the students, including my sister, had ended up there after being expelled from more fashionable prep schools. My parents were away, as they were every weekend, at the farm in Virginia. I was in France on a student trip. Gordon was spending the summer in Boston. Before heading downtown, Jennie had taken LSD. At the rally, she met up with a young man and brought him home to my parents' house. Jennie eventually fell asleep, and the young man left, taking all my mother's jewelry in his knapsack. ("I told him he could take *one* thing," Jennie told me much later.)

When my parents returned to the city Sunday evening, Jennie was psychotic. They committed her to a mental hospital where she stayed on and off for many months. She and my parents endured weekly family counseling sessions in which she laid bare the facts of my mother's drunken rages. In those days, mental health professionals liked to blame bad parenting for all sorts of adolescent problems. Suddenly, my mother's drinking was the focus of everyone's attention. The connection between her drinking and my sister's psychosis was assumed and unquestioned. My mother had always expressed contempt for doctors and anything that smacked of "head shrinking." She denied everything. The hospital staff took her prickly defensiveness as further evidence of her guilt. My mother usually came home from the sessions in tears. Her alcoholism was now a family matter. The toothpaste was out of the tube.

Jennie recovered over the course of several months. But her relationship with my mother did not. Till her dying day, my mother never forgave her, either for outing her as an abusive alcoholic, or for the theft of her jewelry, valuable family heirlooms that were never recovered. She often tormented Jennie by presenting me with an exquisite piece of her mother's jewelry that had been kept in a safety deposit box. "Jennie's already gotten *hers*," she would snarl. My mother's blatantly preferential treatment of me all but shipwrecked my sisterly bond with Jennie, which had been extremely tight. It took many years for Jennie to swallow her resentment and for me to assuage my survivor's guilt. But the scar tissue is still there, and sometimes it feels very tender. All that submerged family history surfaced in my mind as

I listened to Helen Louise and Blake chat about the Kirbys' martini habit. Helen Louise insisted that I keep the letter. I pulled myself from the undertow of those roiling memories and stashed it in my notebook.

Moore's visits to Hooper Bald became less frequent. In his absence, Cotton McGuire and the hunting guides kept Moore's guests entertained. But conditions at the lodge were difficult. The hot water system was finicky. Winters were very cold, and the pipes would freeze and break, requiring McGuire's constant attention. Unlike the boars, other animals fared poorly on Hooper Bald. Within a few years, the buffalo herd died off. The number of mule deer also dwindled, and poachers bagged most of the game birds. By the early 1920s, my grandfather owed Cotton McGuire many thousands of dollars in back pay. He had not been to Hooper Bald for more than a year. He summoned McGuire to New York, where he handed him $1,000 in cash and the lease to Hooper Bald. "It's all yours," he said.

Although Moore left few human traces on Hooper Bald, his short-lived hunting preserve has left a dubious legacy throughout the country. The boars that escaped from Hooper Bald bred with local wild hogs and their population quickly spread into Tennessee and Georgia. Likewise, the progeny of the Russian boars that Moore would introduce a decade later at his Rancho San Carlos in California roamed far beyond Carmel, breeding with wild hogs and colonizing the entire state of California. To this day, wild boars are a scourge to farmers and landowners—to virtually everyone except a handful of big game hunters who live for the thrill of taking them down. In closing his letter to Stuyvie, my grandfather evoked a scene that might have occurred in *Citizen Kane*:

"The last time I saw William Randolph Hearst, Sr., he said, 'your pigs have reached San Simeon.'"

— CHAPTER 9 —

London Calling

WHEN JAY GATSBY tells Nick Carraway that he was honored in World War I by all the Allied countries after making a heroic stand in the Argonne Forest, Nick suspects that the story is another of Gatsby's fantastical self-inventions. But when Gatsby pulls from his pocket a medal he received from Montenegro inscribed "Major Jay Gatsby—For Valour Extraordinary," Carraway swallows his skepticism. "To my astonishment, the thing had an authentic look." My grandfather also played a role in the war. Like Nick, I was incredulous when I first read his account of his wartime experiences. And, like Nick, I was astonished to discover that Moore's stories are corroborated by many sources. His service, if you could call it that, was unorthodox, to say the least.

It was Moore's friendship with a woman named Emilie Grigsby that set him on his meandering path to the general headquarters of the British Expeditionary Forces at the start of World War I. Grigsby could have stepped out of an Edith Wharton novel. She was born into a well-to-do Kentucky family in 1876 and was being raised as a proper Southern belle when her father, an army colonel, died unexpectedly, leaving the family penniless. Lacking any marketable skills, her mother took Emilie and her brother to Cincinnati and opened a brothel.

Grigsby was an early blooming beauty. As a teenager, she caught the eye of Charles T. Yerkes, an American streetcar baron not unlike my grandfather. Yerkes was married, but he brought Grigsby to New York, where she became his mistress. Yerkes provided for her generously, giving her a sumptuously furnished mansion on Park Avenue and jewelry and art worth millions of dollars, including paintings by Corot and Monet. The mansion was known in the neighborhood as the "House of Mystery." It contained several false doors and secret passageways as well as a hidden elevator that brought Yerkes from the basement to Emilie's love nest on the top floor. The lovers publicly maintained that she was his legal ward and that her riches had sprung from an enormous inheritance back in Kentucky.

Yerkes died in 1905, leaving his wife mired in litigation over his gargantuan debts. Much to the widow's fury, Grigsby owned the Park Avenue house, its art, and her jewelry free and clear. Shunned by New York high society because of her relationship with Yerkes and her mother's scandalous vocation, Grigsby sold her mansion and its contents and moved to London. "Fifth and Madison Avenue may be closed to me," she announced, "but I'm young, pretty, and there are other worlds to conquer." She settled in a Mayfair townhouse where she cultivated a salon of writers, artists, and celebrities who were delighted by her sophisticated American tastes and wayward past. The group included Moore, another newcomer on the London scene.

In the summer of 1910, Moore was back in the United States looking after his business interests when he received a letter from Grigsby inviting him to attend a party in New York in honor of her friend Sir John French. French was Inspector General of the British Army and had traveled to Canada that summer to review the troops. Moore declined the invitation. It happened that his horse Justice Brooke was entered to run that weekend in the Kentucky Futurity. "I am not missing the Kentucky Trots for a British General," he told Grigsby.

As it turned out, Moore's meeting with French would come soon enough. In the fall he returned to England on the RMS *Mauretania*. He had noticed that the ship's passenger list included General French and asked the steward in charge of the ship's living room if French happened to be present. The steward directed him to a man sitting nearby. "I introduced myself," wrote my grandfather, "and from that minute we were the best of friends."

Moore's life was filled with providential encounters like this one. But his meeting with French on a transatlantic liner wasn't strictly a matter of serendipity. It was entirely by chance that Grigsby happened to mention General French's name to Moore that summer, but it was no accident that Moore took the crucial next step of seeking him out and introducing himself. Most people live their lives without seeing the opportunities that lie before them, much less seizing them. But Moore was different; he always kept an eye out for the next possible turn of fortune. As it turned out, his meeting with French unlocked the door to many incredible experiences in the years that followed.

Sir John Denton Pinkstone French was handsome and charming. Despite his diminutive stature—he was all of five feet, two inches tall—he was a dynamic officer who had gained distinction as commander of the cavalry division in the second Boer War. When he returned to England from that protracted conflict, he rose quickly through the military ranks. French was a controversial figure. Some of his peers dismissed him as a glory hunter, arguing that his success in Africa was largely fortuitous. Others claimed that his professional advancement was due to the improper influence of certain powerful patrons.

Whatever French's military merits, his titles and honors impressed Moore as much as Moore's wealth and personal style impressed French. Although the general was nearly thirty years Moore's senior, the two men had much in common. They were both of Irish descent; they had a taste for fast horses;

and, as the *New York Times* put it, they shared "a predilection for the aristocracy." They were also shameless skirt-chasers. Sir John had a wife and three children stashed away in the Hertfordshire countryside. Moore had a wife and daughter back in Michigan. But neither man maintained even a veneer of marital fidelity. French's philandering had been widely known since the early 1890s, when he was cited for adultery after having an affair with the wife of a fellow officer in India, an offense that nearly capsized his military career.

Lancaster Gate, c. 1905

French and Moore became virtually inseparable. "When we got to London, we dined together, and every night for two months, adding his social friends and mine, we spent our evenings together," wrote Moore. It wasn't long before Moore suggested that they share a house in London. He found a six-story townhouse at 94 Lancaster Gate, a swank mid-nineteenth-century terrace overlooking Kensington Gardens. Moore outfitted the house with furnishings he bought at auction in a job lot billed as the former "property of a gentleman." Once he and French had settled in, Moore paid all the household expenses, including a staff of twelve servants.

For Sir John, the invitation to share a house in London with a flamboyant American millionaire was too good to pass up. He was not a wealthy man. Several years earlier he had nearly lost his shirt after making bad investments in South African mining interests. But his straitened circumstances did not diminish his expensive tastes. He had a string of mistresses and was always in need of a discreet place to entertain them. Lancaster Gate would be the perfect setting for his trysts.

The domestic plan suited my grandfather equally well. It cemented his friendship with Sir John and enhanced his status among the aristocrats he sought to impress. But most important, through Sir John he became friends with some of the top military men in England, including Winston Churchill, who was then serving as First Lord of the Admiralty. Moore was especially fond of Churchill's "very lovely wife, Clementine." He recalled the "many times we dined with Clemmy and Winston at 11 Downing Street, at which I listened to their discussions for the war that, in my ignorance, I never believed would come." He added, "but there was never any doubt that Sir John and Winston were sure of it."

In the years before the war, Moore and French threw parties at 94 Lancaster Gate that were the height of naughtiness and glamour. An American journalist who visited the house regularly, described it as "something like a salon for the remnants of King Edward VII's old set." At their dinner parties, he wrote, you were likely to meet "anybody who was anybody socially, politically, or artistically." Moore and French were certainly not the only married men in London who stepped out on their wives, but their notorious bachelor pad raised eyebrows and murmurs of disapproval. Sir Henry Wilson, a senior Army staff officer, noted in his diary in 1913: "Dined Johnnie French at 94 Lancaster Gate. An enormous house and what he is doing there I can't think." In 1914, the

Duchess of Rutland went to a dance there and was shocked by the number of unchaperoned women: "GM and Sir J are running a bordello!!!" Neither man seemed to care what people thought. And no one turned down invitations to their parties.

In early 1910, Moore was looking to hire a young man as his secretary. He asked his friend Edward Archibald Hume, a lawyer and diplomat and graduate of Trinity College, Oxford, for help in finding one. Hume responded by sending a letter of inquiry to R.W. Raper, a tutor and fellow at Trinity. The letter described the would-be employer as "an American engaged in some of the largest financial operations in the world and a very rich and successful person (a splendid chance for someone)." The job, continued Hume, called for "a *gentleman* of tact—cheerful and willing and able to write a good letter and frame and transmit important cable messages. A bachelor age about 27–30 but he *must be able to write short hand fairly well*." Hume noted that the short-hand qualification might be a problem but urged Raper to send along the credentials of any possible candidates.

Raper happened to have just the person in mind for the mysterious American business mogul, a student named Guy Charteris. Guy was the youngest son of Hugo Richard Charteris, the eleventh Earl of Wemyss, known as Lord Elcho, one of the most prominent men in England. Raper saw to it that the necessary references were made. Satisfied by Guy's qualifications, and no doubt impressed by his noble lineage, Moore hired him immediately. There's no telling whether Guy was a capable secretary. I can't imagine he had ever heard the word "shorthand." But he and Moore got along well, and the following year Moore took him to the United States for several months to take care of various business matters.

Moore might not have needed Guy's assistance, but he was proud to show off the young aristocrat to his friends and associates. Guy was living proof of the success of his bold British endeavor.

After returning home to England in the spring of 1912, Guy announced his engagement to Frances Lucy Tennant. Tennant's aunt was Margo Asquith, the wife of Henry Herbert Asquith, Prime Minister of England. Moore insisted on throwing an engagement party for the couple at the new and ostentatiously luxurious Ritz Hotel in Mayfair. Guy and Frances compiled a guest list of more than 200 people. The party was a triumph. "Overnight," Moore later wrote, "I who had no social contacts or pretensions, now knew everyone who really mattered in Mayfair Society." He soon received an invitation from Guy's parents, Hugo and Mary Charteris—Lord and Lady Elcho—to a weekend party at Stanway House, the seat of the Charteris family.

Stanway House, 2006

I spent a morning at Stanway House in June 2014 at the invitation of James Charteris, the present Lord Wemyss. Stanway, a honey-colored Jacobean manor house in the Cotswolds, is notable for its architecture: steep peaked gables, tall, clustered chimneystacks, and a gatehouse with whimsical curvilinear gables crowned with scallop shells that look like a row of fancy ladies' hats against the skyline. Lord Wemyss, an amiable gray-haired gentleman, greeted me at the door and served me tea in the kitchen. "I apologize your cup is so big," he said, handing me an enormous cup on a matching saucer the size of a dinner plate. I suddenly felt like Alice in Wonderland. The house, like my teacup, had a fantastic, disorienting atmosphere.

After our tea, Lord Wemyss gave me a full tour of the house. He told me many stories about former occupants of Stanway, including the playwright J. M. Barrie, a family friend, who rented the house every summer from 1923 to 1932. "We children had to dress up as Peter Pan whenever he visited," he said, frowning at the recollection. In the great hall, he pointed to places on the ceiling where Barrie had thrown pennies with stamps stuck to them. "Some of them are still there," he told me, although I couldn't see them. Many of the house's furnishings have been there for centuries. The drawing room upstairs contained a shuffleboard table from the time of Charles I, who ruled England from 1625 until his execution in 1649. A table of curiosities held many intriguing objects including a piece of dark-hued marble that had been part of Hitler's desk from the Berlin Chancellery. "One of my relatives brought the desk back after the war," Lord Wemyss explained. "We decided to smash it and give out pieces as souvenirs."

In the extensive acreage behind the house is the ultimate garden folly, a 300-foot tall gravity-fed fountain, the tallest in

England, that Lord Wemyss installed in 2004. The spectacle was magnificent, a giant plume of water shooting into the sky, spinning the midday sunlight into miniature rainbows as it rose to its full height. Other than the addition of the fountain, Lord Wemyss assured me that nothing much has changed at Stanway since my grandfather attended the house party there in September 1912.

— CHAPTER 10 —

Looks, Bloodlines, and Money

Arriving at Stanway House that weekend in his cream-colored Rolls-Royce Silver Ghost, Moore passed through the gatehouse with its scallop shell embellishments. A traditional emblem of pilgrimage, the scallop shell was an auspicious icon for his journey. For the other guests that weekend, Stanway was just another elegant country house where they could amuse and indulge themselves. For Moore, it was the apotheosis of Old World grandeur that he aspired to.

The Charterises were one of England's most elite families. They were original members of "the Souls," a group of late-Victorian aristocrats that included Prime Ministers Arthur James Balfour and Henry Asquith. (The group was named by Lord Charles Beresford, who apparently exclaimed, "You all sit and talk about each other's souls—I shall call you 'the Souls.'") While they may have been preoccupied with their inner lives, the Souls also took a great interest in each other's spouses. Mary Charteris and Balfour were just one of the adulterous couples in the group.

Edwardian house parties encouraged socializing and sport of all kinds, at all hours of the day and night. Indeed, such occasions were often designed to accommodate the desires of wayward husbands and wives. As attentive hosts, Lord and Lady Elcho were careful to arrange bedroom assignments with their guests' amorous preferences in mind. Stanway's floor plan was ideally suited to midnight misbehavior; Lord Wemyss assured me that the house had seen its share. Moore must have hoped to join in some spicy flirtation at Stanway that weekend.

None of the guests appeared to my grandfather more manifestly noble than Henry and Violet Manners, Duke and Duchess of Rutland, and their head-turning daughter, Diana. The Manners family was rich and powerful. Henry and Violet were fellow members of the Souls. An amateur artist and sculptor, Violet was notoriously headstrong and manipulative in her relations with everyone, particularly her husband and children. It was widely known that she had carried on a torrid love affair with Harry Cust, an exceptionally good-looking man who was said to have been Diana's actual father. Diana was fond of Cust and when she learned, in her early twenties, of his alleged paternity she expressed delight at the notion of being "A Living Monument to Incontinence."

Whatever her paternity, Diana Manners was considered the most beautiful woman in England. She had come out in society two years earlier with a formal court presentation at Buckingham Palace. In her teens, Diana was at the center of a group of artistically inclined young aristocrats known as the "Corrupt Coterie." "Our pride," wrote Diana, "was to be unafraid of words, unshocked by drink and unashamed of 'decadence' and gambling." Diana never overtly breached the bounds of decorum, but she tiptoed near the edge. At a charity ball in the Royal Albert Hall she was to be part of a procession of dancing princesses masquerading as glistening white swans, an homage to the celebrated London premiere of the Ballets Russes' *Swan Lake* in June 1910. She arrived at the hall dressed head to toe in black and joined the procession, a black swan among the feathery cloud of swan-princesses. Afterwards, Violet told everyone that "poor little Diana" had to be dressed in black so that she would not outshine the others.

Diana was not a typical beauty. In an era where personal appearance and dress were rigidly conventional, Diana was a self-styled exotic. She shunned ordinary floor-length silk and taffeta dresses, preferring to dress in unusual foreign fashions. Her wardrobe spilled over with long silk robes, loose-fitting peasant shirts, and sandals. One friend described her as "an orchid among cowslips, a black tulip in a garden of cucumbers, nightshade in the day nursery." Such was her celestial presence that the writer Violet Trefusis remarked, "so must the angel have looked who turned Adam and Eve out of the Garden of Eden. With a face like that she should, I thought, carry a sword or trumpet." Diana loved publicity and could never get enough of it. British women's magazines and the newspaper society pages rippled with her latest activities. Everyone clamored for the privilege of entertaining her. The most sought-after guests in England were the Royals, of course, but Diana was the more talked-about prize.

Diana Manners, c. 1917

Diana's two older sisters had satisfied their parents' expectations by marrying wealthy aristocrats; the duchess was determined to steer her youngest daughter into the arms of a suitable young man. The duchess set her sights high; at the top of her list of "eligibles" was the Prince of Wales. But Diana did not care for him and had no desire to become part of the royal family. There were other appropriate young men in the duchess's crosshairs, but none that appealed to Diana. When one of these would-be suitors became engaged to another woman, the duchess drew a skull and crossbones next to his name.

My grandfather was on the hunt that weekend, not only for deep-pocketed investors but also for a new love interest. The wife he had left back in Michigan was beautiful, but she wasn't rich or distinguished. She had been the perfect starter wife for an upstart small-town lawyer. He had provided her with several elegant homes—the St. Clair mansion as well as houses in Port Huron and Detroit—but he had no emotional capital in the relationship. When Moore's fortunes soared, so did his romantic aspirations. With her penetrating blue eyes, wavy halo of golden hair, and silken skin, Diana Manners immediately caught his eye, quickening his imagination and his sporting instincts. She was beautiful and flirtatious. And eligible—at least on paper. That she was entirely out of his league socially only added to her allure. The qualities he sought in a woman were the same qualities he looked for in horses and hunting dogs: good looks, strong bloodlines, and money. Diana had all three.

Moore was a conspicuous figure at Stanway that weekend. His wealth was astonishing, even by the standards of the affluent British aristocrats who poured their money into his investment schemes. Furthermore, he was American, and unmistakably so. Despite his impeccably tailored clothing and affected good manners, he lacked the refinement of the other guests. While some may have disdained his robust, rough-hewn appetites and opinions, he gained everyone's attention. Standing in front of the magnificent fireplace in Stanway's Great Hall, he regaled the party with tales of his hunting preserve in the Smoky Mountains and his far-flung travels in South America and Canada. He was nothing if not original in his endeavors. Diana Manners was intrigued by the brash outsider. Moore was a refreshing change from the ordinary English gentlemen she had come to find tiresome. She described him in her memoir as "a most unusual man of thirty-six, Red Indian in appearance with straight black hair, flattened face and atomic energy." Although he was nearly twice her age, his passion for the new and unusual made him a kindred spirit of sorts.

In my mother's disarray of photographs and scrapbooks there was a pastel sketch of a woman's face in profile, her blonde hair tied back loosely with a pale blue scarf. When I was eight or nine, I asked my mother if this was a picture of my grandmother. She had died a couple of years before I was born and I had never seen a picture of her, although I understood that she had been a beauty. No, said my mother, this was not my grandmother, but a woman named Diana Manners, who had been a friend of her father's from long ago.

I quizzed my mother about what it meant to be beautiful. At that age, I believed beauty was a yes or no proposition: either you were beautiful or you weren't. What I remember most vividly about that conversation was my mother's pronouncement that beautiful women always had long necks. Women with average—or God forbid, short—necks were out of luck in the beauty department. I asked my mother hopefully if I had a long neck. Her equivocal response signaled to me that I was destined to a life of plainness. I was devastated. Looking back on this exchange now, I think my mother was probably not passing judgment on my looks but on my vanity. She scorned vanity and condemned obvious displays of self-adornment as vulgar. She herself was an attractive woman, more handsome than beautiful, with high cheekbones, a passably long neck, and clear blue eyes. She dressed conservatively and always wore a string of pearls with matching earrings and a muted shade of pink lipstick. The more I learned about my grandmother, a self-obsessed glamour-puss, the more I came to understand the source of my mother's ambivalence about beauty.

I always resented Diana because of her enviable swanlike neck. I still have the sketch, which somehow survived my parents' house fire. It is inscribed "Diana VR, 1915, sitting to Belgian sculptor Rousseau," presumably a preparatory drawing by Diana's mother, Violet Rutland (VR), for a bust of Diana commissioned by my grandfather. A few years ago I had coffee with Diana's granddaughter, Artemis Cooper, in London. I asked her if the statue was ever made, but she didn't know.

On December 4, 1912, it was reported in the *Washington Post* that "George Gordon Moore of New York gave a dinner at the Ritz last night which in magnificence and sumptuousness has never been surpassed in the history of brilliant entertainments held in that smart hotel." The dinner took place in the ballroom, which, despite the season, had been converted into a flower garden. The flowers alone would have cost more than $63,000 in today's currency. The guests received extravagant party favors, including, for the women, "mandarin oranges in each of which was enclosed a gold box filled with bonbons." During the dinner, the guests were entertained from two stages, "on one of which was a troupe of Negro singers, while from the opposite side of the ballroom an orchestra discoursed music at intervals." After dinner, the ballroom was cleared, and at eleven o'clock dancing began.

Moore invited many prominent people, including Lord and Lady Elcho and Prime Minister Asquith. But the guest of honor—and the only one who truly mattered to him—was Diana Manners. He seated the young beauty next to him at the table, making his amorous intentions evident to all. When the orchestra struck up the dance music—American ragtime was all the rage in London at the time—Moore insisted on spinning Diana around the dance floor. On that magical night at the Ritz, the stars in Moore's firmament aligned: the son of dirt-poor Irish immigrants held in his arms the most coveted English rose.

After Moore's party at the Ritz, he courted Diana, as she put it, "in his own exaggerated way." Moore let her know that she was unique among the scores of lovely young women he knew; he told her that she "penetrated his consciousness." Moore did not consider his wife and daughter in America an impediment to his pursuit of Diana. "He gave me to understand that these hindrances could be liquidated and that his every living hour and his vast fortune would be dedicated to me—to me and Sir John French," she wrote. Although Diana did not take Moore seriously as a suitor, she was flattered by his attention. She reveled in his unusual American tastes and his boundless generosity and capacity for pleasure. "He moved in a shower of gold," she wrote. "He doled it out on the just and unjust and on his whims."

Diana was, of course, the primary beneficiary of Moore's largesse, which she accepted with alacrity. His gifts included a gigantic sapphire said to have belonged to Catherine the Great, "a monstrous little monkey called Armide with a diamond waist belt and chain," and a "cream poodle called Fido cut *en papillon* with pompons and bracelets of fluff and a heliotrope bow." Every week he sent what she described as "coffin-sized" boxes of Madonna lilies to her door. Hoping to impress her with his intellectual and sexual sophistication, he gave her Morocco-bound books by two famously promiscuous writers, Guy de Maupassant and Moore's presumed namesake, George Gordon, Lord Byron. Before presenting her with a fur coat, he asked the duchess's advice. She carefully examined the offerings at Swan & Edgar's, London's most stylish furrier, before choosing a floor-length ermine.

If the duchess had kept a list of ineligibles, Moore would no doubt have been at the very top. He had no title, not even a flashy New World pedigree. His origins were unknown and rumors about him spread through the drawing rooms of Mayfair. The duke and duchess referred to him as "Little Big Head" because of his "Red Indian" appearance. "Married!! And black blood!!!" the duchess exclaimed to her brother, Charlie. No one knew for certain how Moore had made his fortune. People referred to him as the "mysterious American millionaire" and the "Michigander promoter." His shadowy past invited speculation that he was a con man. Diana recalled rumors that he "couldn't show his face in New York." "His riches were evident but maybe an optical illusion," she wrote, "so his countrymen said. Harsh things they whispered—'Kicked out of the States,' 'Just a crook.'" But despite his sketchy reputation, Moore had many admirers in England. "We all believed in him," wrote Diana.

As I explored my grandfather's headlong pursuit of Diana Manners, I was struck by the parallels to Jay Gatsby's wooing of Daisy Buchanan. Here were two social nobodies with unsavory backgrounds and endless amounts of cash desperately trying to win the hearts of well-bred goddesses. Unlike Gatsby, Moore could not purchase a mansion within sight of Diana's door, but he did the next best thing: he threw a party at the Ritz. Moore could have chosen another chic hotel such as the Savoy or Claridge's, but the Ritz was practically in Diana's backyard. It was, in fact, visible from her family's house on Arlington Street. For Moore, the hotel fulfilled the same grand purpose as Gatsby's gaudy Franco-American mansion. The lamps illuminating the gatehouse at

16 Arlington Street were Moore's equivalent of the green light at the end of Daisy Buchanan's dock.

A month after the celebrated party at the Ritz, society columns announced Moore's impending marriage to Diana. Typical was the report in the *Indianapolis Star*: "It is rumored in London that Lady Diana Manners, the only unmarried daughter of the Duke and Duchess of Rutland, is about to become the bride of George Gordon Moore, an American financier. Mr. Moore has spent much time in her company since the holidays." A gossip columnist writing under the name of Lady Mary Manwaring wrote a cattier version of the engagement. "Rumor is . . . busily coupling [Moore's] name with the pretty daughter of one of London's loveliest women," she wrote. "Mr. Moore is of average height, with broad shoulders that make him look shorter than he really is, keen dark eyes, and a chin that seems to indicate that, if he made up his mind to marry the young lady in question, he will do it, no matter what her reputation for willfulness may be."

Given her distaste for Moore, the Duchess of Rutland must have found these rumors annoying. But the war was to make strange bedfellows. By October 1914, she was reconsidering Moore as a mate for her youngest daughter.

— CHAPTER 11 —

"War is Certain. Come at Once."

As CHILDREN, MY SIBLINGS AND I were never included in our parents' dinner parties (nor did we want to be). So we were never present when my grandfather, during his Christmas visits, entertained my parents and their guests with tales of his adventures in World War I. I remember my father's dismissive suggestion that the old man's stories were greatly embellished, something along the lines of "He said he was friends with Winston Churchill, but he probably just shook his hand once or twice." It turns out my father was wrong.

Moore might not have believed that war would come, but the possibility exhilarated him. What he knew about war came from vivid accounts in works such as Caesar's *Gallic Wars* and in the tabloid newspaper reports of the Spanish-American War. Moore had probably heard the opinion voiced by some Englishmen that war would be good for a country they believed had gone soft and spoiled. H. G. Wells, for example, rejoiced that a new "heroic age" had arrived. "No legendary fears of the past," he wrote, "no battle with dragons or monstrous beasts, no quest or fear that man has hitherto attempted can compare with this adventure, in terror, danger and splendour."

Moore also drew his notions of battle from the sport of polo. He enjoyed the spectacle of aristocratic athletes galloping their nimble ponies up and down a field that was as smooth and green as a billiard table. I think he imagined that wartime battles would resemble polo on a grander scale, with men trading their mallets for sabers and rifles to engage in audacious acts of chivalry. A year earlier, he had told Sir John that he wanted to see a battle firsthand. His friend assured him that he might get his wish soon enough. War was not simply pageantry for Moore. For wealthy businessmen like him, war meant money. He had invested heavily in railroads and power companies, interests that stood to profit monumentally if mobilized for the war effort. How could such an insatiable capitalist not be excited by the prospect of the European conflict? Moore spent the summer of 1914 in San Francisco, working on a multimillion-dollar deal backed by British investors to purchase and reorganize the United Properties Company, a colossal amalgamation of public transportation systems.

Every day, Moore pored over newspapers for signs of international instability. The headlines that summer were particularly ominous: war in the Balkans, competition for access to Persian oilfields, negotiations between England and Germany over control of the Berlin-Baghdad Railway. Although he had earlier doubted that England would go to war, he was not entirely surprised when, in late July, his British investors withdrew their capital and tanked the United Properties deal. His suspicions about the war were confirmed days later when he received a cable from Sir John French, who was about to be appointed commander-in-chief of the British Expeditionary Force in Europe. French's message was simple: "War is Certain. Come at Once." England officially declared war on August 4, 1914.

After receiving French's summons, Moore booked passage from New York to Liverpool. On the way east, he stopped in Michigan to check on his hottest racing prospect, a lightning-fast two-year-old colt he had named General French in honor of his good friend. The colt had yet to race, but Moore expected him to triumph at the track, just as he expected Sir John to triumph on the battlefield.

Field Marshal Sir John French

Moore sailed from New York on September 19 aboard the SS *St. Louis*. Always eager to make new connections, he struck up an acquaintance in the ship's smoking room with a young American named Will Irwin, a freelance war correspondent. Irwin had begun his reporting career in 1901 at the *San Francisco Chronicle* and, in 1904, moved to New York to work for the *New York Sun*. Two years later, he made a name for himself reporting absentee about the San Francisco earthquake of 1906. He knew the city so well that he was able to cobble together vivid reports about the quake and the ensuing fires that devastated the city.

When the war broke out in August 1914, Irwin had been one of the first American correspondents to sail for Europe. He told Moore that he was making his second attempt to get to the front and was not optimistic about his chances. In

"War is Certain. Come at Once."

August, hoping to cover the impending German attack on the Belgian university town of Louvain, he had been turned away by a German officer who warned him that he would be executed if he did not leave immediately. Several days later, on his way to Holland, his train stopped at Louvain as the conflagration there was reaching its height. German soldiers ordered him at gunpoint to remain on board, from where he could see the destruction of houses as well as the execution of defenseless civilians. The experience clinched his determination to cover the war.

Irwin was hugely impressed by what he called Moore's "social talent" and the depth of Moore's knowledge about the lead-up to the war. "Without swank," wrote Irwin, Moore dropped the names of key figures in British politics and society. Perhaps to prove his bona fides, Moore brought Irwin to his cabin late one night and showed him several cables that French had sent him before he sailed from New York. Irwin was amazed by what he read. "Expressed in terms of friendly intimacy," he wrote, "they begged Mr. Moore to come as soon as possible to British headquarters—'I need your support and advice,' read one of them, or words to that effect." To Irwin, Moore seemed "almost too good to be true." But, he added, "he was true." Moore and Irwin parted ways when the *St. Louis* docked in Liverpool. But they had not seen the last of each other. Eventually, Moore would call on Irwin to assist him in an endeavor that Irwin described as "the most bizarre adventure of my life."

After a few days in London, Moore sailed to Boulogne, where he was greeted by French's personal chauffeur, a handsome young man named John Armstrong "Chips" Drexel, a grandson of Anthony J. Drexel, the pioneering financier from Philadelphia. Drexel drove Moore in one of French's two Rolls-Royces to GHQ, a compound that consisted of several houses and chateaus in and around the village of St. Omer. They arrived at Sir John's quarters, a flamboyantly decorated house belonging to a local official, where Drexel showed Moore to his private rooms.

Moore could not have imagined a more perfect guide at the front than Chips Drexel. Already a record-setting aviator at age twenty-three, Drexel had sangfroid to spare. With Sir John's encouragement, Moore and Drexel went wherever they pleased. In November 1914, when British forces moved against the Germans in the ancient Belgian city of Ypres, the two Americans found themselves in the crossfire, with German shells flying all around them. The battle left my grandfather giddy with excitement; he pronounced it "the greatest battle ever fought since Waterloo." He believed that the British victory at Ypres had put a decisive end to the German advance. Such was the naïve optimism that prevailed in the first months of the war.

When Moore arrived at GHQ it was clear that Sir John needed his help. As the commander-in-chief had soon learned, the British army lacked effective weapons to combat the Germans in the new and unfamiliar trench warfare. The Germans had been preparing for war for over a decade, and they were well stocked with armaments. Not only was British ammunition scarce, much of it was defective. The army's hand grenades and shells routinely failed to explode. Some shells were later discovered to contain sawdust. The shoddiness of British weaponry was a source of humiliation; according to historian Richard Holmes, their first flare pistols "were so few in number and limited in effect that their firing drew derisive applause from the enemy trenches." Members of Parliament visited French at the front, and although he complained to them about the shortage of serviceable guns and ammunition, they gave him no assurance that the situation would be remedied. French also sent detailed reports to Lord Kitchener, Secretary of State for War, about the Germans' use of new mechanical inventions such as grenade launchers and high explosives. He lamented that the War Office received his pleas "with a carelessness which bordered on incredulity."

Having been told essentially to make do, French asked Moore to set up a field site for developing new weaponry. He considered Moore his closest friend in the world and believed in Moore's passionate support of the Allies. Moore saw the weapons shortage as an eminently solvable problem. As he liked to say, "Trouble-shooting is my business." Moore commandeered property in the town of Helfaut, four miles south of St. Omer, for a weapons laboratory. Although he knew nothing about arms and ammunition, he happened to know a couple of Americans who were experts in the field. In 1912, on a business trip to California, Moore had met William Lawrence "Billie" Breese, a colorful character and just the sort of enterprising businessman Moore admired. Moore knew that Breese had come to Europe in 1913 to help a retired U.S. Army colonel named Isaac Newton Lewis market his recent invention, a lightweight machine gun. (Later known as the "Lewis gun," this was to become one of most effective weapons of twentieth-century warfare.) Moore tracked down Breese and Lewis in Belgium and brought them to Helfaut to advise him on the armaments problem.

With Lewis's help, the Helfaut site soon began to experiment with new weapons such as rocket launchers and flame projectiles. While some of its early efforts failed, the weapons laboratory was surprisingly effective. Within a few months, the operation was officially designated a Special Company under the direction of Major C. H. Foulkes of the Army Corps of Royal Engineers. Sir John took a great interest in the project and monitored its progress closely. "Under Mr. Moore's advice and direction, experiments were carried out with the maximum of speed, energy, and resource," he later wrote, "and a number of factories and small plants were set up for the production, for use in the field, of properly constructed hand-grenades, bombs, and trench mortars." During the remainder of French's tenure as commander-in-chief, which lasted until November 1915, the British Expeditionary Force would produce more mortar bombs and grenades at Helfaut than it received from England.

Billie Breese was ready to throw his all-American know-how behind the Allied cause. Although he had no training or experience in engineering, he was keen on explosives. At Moore's urging, he remained at Helfaut into the following year to assist in developing and producing ammunition. One of the operation's primary objectives was to devise an explosive more powerful than shrapnel. The British had used shrapnel successfully in the Boer Wars, and Lord Kitchener insisted that it would be adequate for the war in Europe. But shrapnel shells were practically useless against the Germans' dense barbed-wire barricades. In the words of one British officer, shrapnel was "of about as much use against intrenched troops as a basket of tennis balls." The only ammunition capable of penetrating the German barricades was the high explosive shell, of which British troops had very few.

Breese was determined to develop an explosive that could blast through the Germans' seemingly impregnable barricades. Through trial and error, he put together a device powerful enough to do the job. On a Sunday afternoon in March, a group of British officers gathered at Helfaut to watch Breese show off his newfangled weapon. Valentine Williams, a young foreign correspondent for the *Daily Mail*, accompanied my grandfather to Helfaut to watch the demonstration. Williams's experience at Helfaut that day lodged my grandfather forever in his memory.

Breese's weapon consisted of a rocket separated by a piece of iron called a *sabot* from a charge of thirty-five pounds of explosive material packed in a pear-shaped container of light metal. The weapon was mounted on a tripod installed in a trench and fired with a lanyard. "Breese would pull the string, with an eerie, piercing shriek the rocket would shoot upward in a high parabola and drop to earth," wrote Williams. "There would be a few seconds' impressive silence, then an ear-shattering roar and a great spout of earth." He remarked that the process was "far from perfect" and that charges often failed to explode. He described Breese as a reckless fellow who often used a corkscrew to remove the detonators for repeated use. Despite the danger, Williams had stayed with Breese in the trench all afternoon, sometimes pulling the lanyard to set off the rocket blast.

As the afternoon light began to fade the audience dispersed, leaving only Williams, Moore, and a few casual spectators. There was only one projectile remaining. As Williams stood in the trench waiting for Breese to pull the lanyard, Moore called out, "Oh, Williams, just a minute!" Williams turned around to see Moore standing on high ground, thirty yards or so from where he and Breese stood. He climbed out of the trench and walked toward Moore. "I had not gone half a dozen yards when my ears were deafened, the ground shook with a terrific explosion," he recalled. "I swung about. Breese and his gun had disappeared. Where they had been a cloud of black smoke mushroomed into the air. I ran forward. I found Breese some yards along the trench where he had been blown, dead, with his head shattered." Williams later learned that Breese had forgotten to insert the iron sabot separating the rocket and charge so that when the rocket was fired, it prematurely detonated the charge. He wrote, "If George Moore had not spoken an instant before, I should have suffered his friend's fate. Standing there, with the reek of high explosive in my nostrils, I felt as though Death had brushed my sleeve in passing."

Moore returned to St. Omer blood-stained and badly shaken. The next day he reported the tragedy to Sir John who, in turn, reported it in a letter to a friend. "A horrible thing happened yesterday about which I only heard of this morning," he wrote. "After I left him at h.q. George went out to the ground where weapons were being tested. There was an explosion. His friend Breeze [sic] was killed instantly. George was standing near and I hear he was knocked down by the blast of it. Poor boy he is horribly cut up. He went back this morning. So this day which began in calm ended in storm."

Breese was killed on March 14, 1915, just as the Battle of Neuve Chappelle had begun. When the War Office released news of his death, it withheld the true cause, claiming instead that Breese was killed in action when the British forces stormed Neuve Chappelle. The War Office had ample reason to cover up the truth. Kitchener's staff preferred that the Breese family believe that their beloved Billie had died in combat rather than in a reckless mishap behind the lines. And the War Office did not want anyone to know that, out at the front, Moore and Breese—a couple of Americans who had no business being there—were secretly involved in developing weapons that the War Office had not been able to provide.

What was an American maverick like my grandfather doing at the front? French provided him with comfortable quarters at GHQ and encouraged him to attend all meetings and battle conferences whenever he came to visit. When pressed, French described Moore as his personal assistant. Moore claimed to have been offered the position of colonel, which would have made him subject to the orders of all superior officers. He declined, explaining that "if I remained in mufti, or plain clothes, the only one I would take orders from would be Sir John French. I preferred the mufti."

Few people at GHQ or elsewhere knew that French had charged Moore with setting up the weapons lab at Helfaut. Even fewer knew that another of Moore's secret responsibilities was to act as courier between French and Winifred Bennett, a London socialite unhappily married to a well-known British diplomat. French insisted that Moore have lunch with

Bennett whenever he was in London, so that Moore could return to GHQ armed with her letters as well as news of her appearance, her attire, and the colorful goings-on at Lancaster Gate. "I love seeing dear old George because he always talks of you," wrote French to his beloved. French signed his letters "Peter Pan" to "Wendy Darling." (J. M. Barrie's characters from *Peter Pan, or the Boy Who Wouldn't Grow Up*, were very much in the public eye in those years.)

Several American newspapers reported that Moore's peculiar status at GHQ was causing "criticism and wonderment" across England. This hardly described the vexation of many civilian and military officials who knew of Moore's playboy reputation and resented his intimate relationship with Sir John. The *Washington Post* reported that Moore stayed with French in "a handsome chateau, characterized by sumptuous lounging rooms, with pink and gold furnishings and a too careful observance of the refinements of life." According to the *New York World,* much gossip involved the extraordinary privileges Moore enjoyed at the front. "Moore can come and go at his own sweet will," the paper reported, "and can bring along his friends, especially his women friends, just as he chooses." A vitriolic columnist complained of Moore's unlimited access to confidential military information: "Probably there are not half-a-dozen Englishmen, including the Cabinet, who know so much of the inner secrets of the campaign as this American from nowhere."

There were other complaints about French's management of GHQ. In the spring of 1915, his detractors claimed he maintained an unnecessarily large staff of young British bluebloods who spent too much time handicapping horse races and playing bridge until the early hours of the morning. It was further alleged that there were "numerous ladies of high degree, and some not so high, at the field-marshal's headquarters." General Horace Smith-Dorrien, who was known to have an acrimonious relationship with the commander-in-chief, famously scolded Sir John, saying, "Too many whores around your headquarters, Field-Marshal!"

Indifferent to the criticism, or perhaps even amused by it, Moore reveled in the bustling atmosphere at GHQ. Winston Churchill visited several times a month. "I sat regularly at dinner with him," Moore recalled, "and after everyone had left the table, we continued our talks." Moore also became acquainted with the young Prince of Wales. In November, King George had arranged for the prince to serve on Sir John's staff at GHQ, where he would be out of harm's way. The prince occupied the bedroom next to Moore, and Moore was aware of his comings and goings as well as his personal habits. "At about 5 o'clock every morning," wrote Moore, "I could hear him with his servant, who would drop him in his tin bathtub."

Like everyone else at GHQ, the Prince of Wales was aware of Moore's close friendship with the commander-in-chief. The prince wanted very much to leave GHQ and serve in combat with his regiment, the Grenadier Guards. But the king had refused to put him at risk. Frustrated by this unwanted coddling, the prince asked Moore for help in persuading his father to change his mind. Moore was more than happy to oblige. Moore told French about the prince's wishes; when the two men traveled to London in early January 1915, French went directly to Buckingham Palace to pay his respects to King George. When French arrived later at Lancaster Gate, he told Moore that the prince was free to join his regiment. French happily explained how he had managed to convince the king to send his eldest son into combat where he risked being killed. Knowing that King George hated the Kaiser, French told him that the Kaiser had been behaving badly by keeping his sons away from danger at the front lines. French suggested the king could show up the Kaiser's cowardice by sending one of his own sons into combat. According to French, the king replied, "Sir John, no

"War is Certain. Come at Once."

one ever presents anything to me properly. The prince can join his regiment."

That night Moore sent a letter to the Prince of Wales telling him he was free to join the Grenadier Guards. The war was to provide Moore with further opportunities to call in favors and also to grant them.

— CHAPTER 12 —

A Mother's Meddling

WHEN DIANA MANNERS was two years old, Haddon, the older of her two brothers, died suddenly, under mysterious circumstances. He was nine years old and apparently in good health. His parents were secretive about the cause of his death, telling the press and everyone else that he had died of tuberculosis. Although the truth was never publicly disclosed, shortly after Haddon's death, the duchess hinted at the cause in a letter to her close friend Mary Wemyss. "So well," she wrote. "Never ill. And it was just only a tiny acrobatic trick that twisted something inside." The accident occurred on the birthday of his brother John, and it might have been that Haddon was performing for his younger brother. Naturally, the Manners family was devastated by the loss of their first-born son. But the full significance of the tragedy only became apparent twenty years later, in August 1914, when England entered the war against Germany, and John Manners, the family's only remaining heir, enlisted in the army.

Under British laws of inheritance, the Manners fortune was to pass to the closest male descendent of the Duke of Rutland. If John were to die young and without an heir, the dukedom and all the family's property would pass out of the family's direct line, and the line, which traced back to the reign of William the Conqueror, would come to an end.

Violet Manners was determined to prevent the family's only direct heir from risking his life in battle. In *The Secret Rooms*, a chronicle of the wartime escapades of the Manners family, author Catherine Bailey detailed the desperate measures Violet took to keep John out of harm's way. The duchess's dastardly machinations could have been the subject of a tawdry Italian opera in which George Moore had a starring role.

John was dark-haired, slim, and good-looking, but his temperament was subdued and withdrawn—the opposite of his sister Diana. By Bailey's reckoning, this was due not to nature but nurture, or a lack thereof, by his parents. Bailey attributed their neglect to a combination of grief and unresolved anger at John for being responsible in some unexplained way for his brother's fatal accident. When Haddon was buried with full fanfare at Belvoir Castle, John was not permitted to attend the funeral. Instead, that same day, his parents dispatched him to boarding school. He was eight years old. He did abominably in school, complaining that the work was too difficult for him. At age thirteen, he went to Eton, and later to Trinity College, Cambridge, from which he graduated in 1908. According to Bailey, from the time John left for boarding school, he lived under the care of Violet's bachelor brother, Charlie Lindsay, the only family member he felt close to.

After college, John's parents arranged for him to serve as honorary attaché to the British Embassy in Rome. A month after his arrival in Italy, the ambassador's wife, a family friend, wrote to Violet about John's comportment. She praised John's charming manners and thoughtfulness, but added that he was not socially inclined, smoked excessively, and refused to learn Italian. John sent letters almost daily to his Uncle Charlie expressing his distaste for his job. So informed, Charlie took it upon himself to explain to Violet that John had no appetite for the diplomatic life.

John's stint in Rome was made even more unpleasant by a disturbing development at home. According to Bailey,

John's father was concerned about family finances and tried to rob John of a substantial piece of his inheritance, a property called Haddon Hall. The plot ultimately failed, but John never forgave his family for this chicanery. After two miserable years in Rome, John returned to England in 1911 and settled in Charlie's house in London.

In the summer of 1914, John enlisted with his regiment, the Leicesters, and was made a lieutenant in the North Midlands Division. When war broke out, the duke and duchess were faced with the very real possibility that their sole heir might be killed in action. They begged him to seek out a position far from the battlefield. They repeatedly recited the devastating effect his death would have on the family and its venerable lineage. But he felt only bitterness for his parents and insisted that his moral obligation was not to his family but to his country.

John was appointed aide-de-camp to General Stuart "Eddy" Wortley, a friend of the Manners family who had assured the duchess that the division would remain in England for at least a few months. But in late August he informed her that his division would be "over the water in 6 weeks' time." In a panic, she wrote to Charlie, "now what can you and I do *secretly*—think and tell me? Surely J could go on the staff of someone *remaining* here to *teach* new army? Think hard—I am up to *anything* secret."

At this point Charlie felt he had no choice but to quietly support Violet's efforts without John's knowledge. Over the next several weeks, the imperious duchess reached out to all the highly ranked officers she knew, but her letters went unanswered. In desperation, she finally wrote to Lord Kitchener, hoping that he might place John on his staff. In a hastily scribbled note, he expressed concern but offered no help. His response enraged her.

The duchess then seized on a different approach. Although John had already been cleared by the medical examiners to serve in combat, Violet insisted that he be examined again

A Mother's Meddling

by a doctor in London. She persuaded the doctor to fail him on the pretense that he had a weakened heart. The doctor agreed to issue the fraudulent report. When John discovered the ruse he was furious. He told General Wortley about the bogus medical examination and asked him to quash the report. Wortley had no patience for Violet's meddling with his personal military staff. He made sure that the report was disposed of.

By October it was clear to Violet that she could not prevent John from going to France. But she was determined that he should remain far from the battlefield and set her sights on a position at GHQ with Sir John French. It was no secret to her or anyone else that French's closest confidant was George Moore, Diana's American suitor. With Moore in mind, Violet settled on a plan.

The duchess had strongly disapproved of Moore and wanted Diana to have nothing to do with him. But if anyone had Sir John's ear, it was Moore. Given Moore's infatuation with Diana, Violet hoped that the right inducements would persuade him to intervene with Sir John on her behalf. Suddenly, Little Big Head became a regular guest at 16 Arlington Street. When the duchess presented her scheme to Diana, the young woman was distraught. In a letter to her sister Marjorie in November, Diana wrote, "Mother . . . says I must make nice to GM. If I won't J will die."

What had the duchess asked Diana to do? "Make nice to" could mean anything from coy flirtation to full-blown seduction. Diana claimed to have abhorred the prospect of cozying up to Moore, but she understood that John was the family's only remaining heir and that he would most likely be killed in combat. Bailey concedes that it's unclear what was promised to Moore, if anything. In any case, it's unlikely that he needed any such inducement to help the duchess in her plight. A confidential request from such a powerful woman made him feel omnipotent. Surely he could persuade his good friend to stash Violet's son safely at GHQ.

Moore approached the duchess's request with the same "trouble-shooting is my business" zeal he applied to every challenge he faced. Helfaut, he concluded, was the ideal place to park John Manners for the duration of the war. In mid-February, he proposed the plan to Sir John and they agreed to go forward with it. Helfaut was to open officially in June, and they decided to wait until then to transfer John to that detail. Sir John immediately wrote a letter to the duchess. "My Dear: Please don't worry yourself or be unhappy," he began. "Trust me to see that he is all right so far as anyone can be so in this kind of a war. Of course, I needn't say how necessary it is for you to keep our correspondence on such a subject absolutely secret. Once he knows of it nothing can be done. But I have a good plan which our mutual friend will explain to you." The mutual friend, of course, was my grandfather.

Violet sent a note to her brother Charlie the morning she received John French's letter regarding the "good plan." In her note she reported having awoken at three o'clock that same morning and gotten up "to see G Moore in Diana's bedroom next door." How exactly did Moore happen to be in the Manners's house at three o'clock in the morning? Had he come to dinner and stayed on after everyone else had gone to bed? Had he escorted Diana home after an evening at the theater? Are we to believe Violet? Is it possible that she fabricated the story after reading Sir John's letter, wishing to believe that the deal she had struck with Moore had been sealed? And if she was telling the truth, what exactly did she see?

We'll never know, although for the sake of a juicy story, Bailey strongly implied that sexual favors were granted, willingly or otherwise. "For understandable reasons, Diana never wrote about what occurred in the early hours of that morning," she wrote. "Whether, as a reward for securing her brother's safety, Moore forced her to submit to his advances, she does not record. But he had evidently extracted some sort of price. For a married man to be found in a debutante's bedroom at that hour broke every convention."

Regardless of what did or did not happen in Diana's bedroom that night, Moore proceeded without delay to get John Manners on board with the Helfaut plan. According to Bailey, he planned a party at Lancaster Gate for Diana and her friends and requested that Diana bring her brother. That evening, Moore seized an opportune moment to take the young man aside. With great excitement, Moore told him about the secret weapons program and asked if he'd be interested in joining the project. Apparently, John was politely enthusiastic in his response, but the next day he complained to his Uncle Charlie that the proposal was ridiculous. Charlie urged him to consider it, invoking the ominous events that would befall the family if he were killed in action. The threats of impecunity and the end of the 900-year family line were a heavy burden for John. But he refused to back down.

The North Midlands Division embarked for Europe in late February. French planned to hold the division back as long as possible. He made clear that North Midlands was not to engage in any action until he issued distinct orders to send them to battle. In mid-March 1915, the disastrous Battle of Neuve Chappelle took a heavy toll on the British army, causing a staffing crisis on the front line. Suddenly it appeared likely that French would send North Midlands into action right away. Moore knew there was no time to lose in getting John Manners to Helfaut.

Although French was preoccupied with the battle's grim aftermath, Moore insisted on meeting with him to set the plan in motion. The two men made their way to Helfaut to consult with the program's chief officer. The recent death of Billie Breese must have caused Moore to doubt the safety of that operation. But it was too late to scuttle the plan. John had already expressed considerable, if feigned, interest in it. And there was no time to come up with an alternative arrangement, given that North Midlands might be called to the front at any moment.

By this time, Sir John French had already come under fire for allowing his American millionaire friend to have unlimited access to GHQ and for choosing his personal staff based on their social standing. Under the circumstances, Moore realized it would be politically disastrous for the commander-in-chief to appoint a socially prominent figure like John Manners, the Marquis of Granby and heir to the Duke of Rutland, to serve with the Special Brigade at Helfaut. Based on his earlier conversation with John, Moore assumed that he would gladly serve there if the opportunity arose. Accordingly, to disguise the true originator of the appointment, he drafted a letter for General French's signature to John's commanding officer, General Wortley. The letter suggested that in light of John's inventiveness and interest in explosives, Wortley might consider sending him to Helfaut.

As soon as the ink was dry, General French's aide-de-camp Lieutenant Colonel Fitzgerald Watt sped off to the North Midlands headquarters to deliver the letter in person. Moore expected that Wortley would raise the question with John and that the young man would eagerly accept the transfer. But things did not go as planned. After Wortley read the letter he handed it to John, saying, "He wants you to go to GHQ. He tells me you're a famous inventor and that you know all about bomb-making. What do you want to do?" John responded, "The Commander-in-Chief must have confused me with someone else. I'm not an inventor and I don't know anything about bombs." Wortley wrote a quick reply politely declining the offer. He gave it to Watt, who hastened back to GHQ with the disappointing news. Word passed quickly from French to Moore that John had refused the Helfaut appointment.

Moore was furious. No doubt he had hesitated before bothering Sir John at that difficult time with a petty personal matter. But for the love of Diana and the good graces of her family he had risked the request. He had come up with what he believed to be a surefire solution. And now the stubborn young officer had refused to play ball. The next morning, Moore summoned Charlie to Lancaster Gate. He did not hide his frustration. "Your boy's failed me. I don't understand it," he told Charlie. "He as good as promised me he would go." But Moore did not let his anger diminish his sense of urgency. He immediately devised a way out of the embarrassing situation John had created. Moore's work-around scheme was utterly preposterous, but cunning, too. Violet's grand plot, which had begun as a stormy Italian opera, suddenly turned into a screwball comedy.

Moore knew it was important for French to save face. He could not simply repeat the invitation once John had refused it. It was necessary to recast the offer in a different light and to persuade John to accept it. Moore's plan was to approach Wortley again, this time in a letter from John's father. With assistance from Violet and Charlie, Moore drafted a letter for the duke's signature explaining that Sir John's letter had contained a clerical error: he had intended to call upon John's interest in *catapults* rather than *explosives*.

At the same time, Charlie wrote to John explaining that the duke was sending Wortley a letter explaining the "clerical error" and expressing concern about the commander-in-chief's hurt feelings. He demanded that John go along with the plan and present himself to French immediately. He instructed him "to take the line that you are far from being an expert, though always interested, and that you are willing to make yourself useful and do all you can with suggestions etc, however little confidence you have in being of use." He continued, "Mr M says that that part is the least to be feared of all. He is convinced that without any real knowledge at all, you are certain to be of use, and I am absolutely certain of it myself. Remember nothing is expected of you." The letter concluded, "This is what I was to tell you, and this is the way

Mr M wants it done if possible. If it can be done without Sir John having to give deliberate orders, it is far best."

John was fed up with his family's pestering. But he knew that further protest would be futile. To placate the family, he agreed to see Sir John although he had no intention of doing so. Moore watched for a message from John Manners to arrive at GHQ, but none came. He knew that Charlie was the only person who might persuade John to join the Special Brigade. In mid-April he advised Charlie that John had not kept his word and implored him to send a more emphatic letter to his nephew. On April 12, Charlie wrote to John:

> I am told to let you have knowledge of the following extract which comes in a letter just received by Mr M from his Great Friend:
> 'Young Granby [one of John Manners's titles] has never shown any sign of coming in to see me yet.'
> You are urged very strongly to write to Brooke [Guy Brooke, aide-de-camp to French] to send for you the moment the Great Friend has time to see you. I feel sure you will understand this and act on it.

But John did not act on it. Within the week, the Allies were engaged in another battle near Ypres. John enjoyed being closer to the action; he watched the combat from a safe position on Scharpenberg Hill and wrote detailed letters to Charlie about the bombs and explosions. The notion of going to Helfaut was less appealing than ever. But his enthusiasm didn't last long.

On April 22, 1915, Moore and Sir John were enjoying a private dinner at GHQ when word arrived that the Germans had released poisonous gas on French and Canadian troops in the Ypres sector. At daybreak the next morning, Sir John sent Moore to drive with his personal physician to Boulogne, site of a Royal Army Medical Corps' hospital, to gather information about the physical effects of the gas.

John Manners witnessed the hideous effects of Germany's chlorine gas attack on the Allied troops. When he returned to headquarters he wrote a letter to his father describing what he had seen:

> When we got to the Hospital, we had no difficulty finding out in which ward the gassed men were, as the noise of the poor devils trying to get breath was sufficient to direct us. . . . There were about twenty men [in the ward], lying on mattresses, and all more or less in a sitting position propped up against the walls. Their faces, arms, hands were of a shiny grey-black colour, with mouths open and lead-glazed eyes, swaying slightly backwards and forwards, trying to breathe.

John understood that press censorship meant that the atrocity he had seen would never be made public. At the close of his letter, he urged his father to have his account published in all the newspapers in England. "Let the truth be known to every man and woman in England," he wrote, "and not hidden under the usual newspaper clouds." A separate letter to his mother made clear how profoundly disturbed John had been by the scene at the hospital. Thoroughly disgusted by the war, he appeared to capitulate on the GHQ matter. "Now about St Omer," he wrote. "I am ready to do what you want simply for your sake, though I expect I should not like it as much, as I have got more or less into this job. Do whatever you yourself want. But remember it must be an order."

In June, John Manners's division was struck by a debilitating stomach virus. Most of the ill were treated on site, but a few, including John, were sent home to recuperate. Although he had reluctantly agreed to quit the front for good, he soon had a change of heart. It appears that he recovered quickly and planned to return to the front at the end of his medical leave. Violet redoubled her efforts, finally persuading the medical board to declare John permanently unfit to serve.

John was despondent over the board's ruling. His mother's schemes had nearly driven him to renounce his family forever. But just then, when the drama seemed destined to end on a bitter note, another operatic twist of fate occurred. A few weeks before Christmas, John fell in love with a beautiful young woman named Kathleen Tennant. Suddenly he could not imagine being away from England for any reason. After a brief, intense courtship, the couple was married on January 27, 1916, in a grand wedding at St. Margaret's Church in Westminster. The *Times* account of the wedding reported that "Lady Diana Manners, who was one of the bridesmaids, designed the bridesmaids' gowns in the medieval manner; they were of white chiffon belted in silver worn with flowing veils of blue tulle held by silver bands." The medieval theme was oddly appropriate for the wedding of a man with an alleged passion for the weaponry of the Middle Ages.

John Manners, 9th Duke of Rutland, and Kathleen Tennant on their wedding day, January 27, 1916

It seems that marriage completely extinguished John Manners's determination to serve on the front line. In December 1915, Sir John French was relieved of his duties in Europe and returned to England to serve as Commander-in-Chief of the Home Forces. The timing could not have been better for Manners. Shortly after his wedding he asked his mother if she might persuade Sir John to give him a position on his staff. Sir John happily obliged, appointing him aide-de-camp, a post he held for the last two and a half years of the war. It's hard to imagine a more perfect ending to the duchess's masterpiece of meddling.

— CHAPTER 13 —

Dances of Death

REGARDLESS OF WHAT TRANSPIRED between Moore and Diana in her Arlington Street bedroom that mysterious night in February 1915, it did not bring an end to their relationship. Diana went to work as a nurse at Guy's Hospital in London, and Moore continued to woo her as the war escalated. He hosted extravagant parties for her at 94 Lancaster Gate, inviting her to draw up the guest list that always included her friends in the "Coterie." Ignoring wartime gloom and austerity, Moore decorated the house for these occasions according to various themes, including the Wild West and the Ballets Russes. Diana's friend Iris Tree described these occasions as "illicit flaming orgies." Her characterization of Moore's parties is borne out by a passage in Diana's memoir. She wrote:

> Parents were excluded. We dined at any time. The long waits for the last-comers were enlivened by exciting, unusual drinks such as vodka or absinthe. The menu was composed of far-fetched American delicacies—avocados, terrapin and soft-shell crabs. The table was purple with orchids. I always sat next to the host, and the dancing, sometimes to two bands, Negro and white (and once to the first

Hawaiian), so that there might be no pause, started immediately after dinner. There were not more than fifty people. We kept whirling to the music till the orchids were swept away in favour of wild flowers, for breakfast eggs and bacon which appeared with the morning light.

The moment Diana left the party, Moore signaled for the band to stop playing and for food and drink to be put away. "When you leave," he told her, "the place is a morgue."

There was a tragic dimension to these wartime parties. Diana called them "dances of death" (a reference to the medieval allegory of Death, in the guise of a skeleton, communing with a group of partygoers and culling some to follow him to the grave). Some of Diana's friends had already been killed in the war. When the lucky survivors came home on leave, Moore held parties in their honor. But every week brought more bad news. Hanging over the festivities was the certainty that some of them would not be seen again. As Diana saw it, she and her friends "were dancing a tarantella frenziedly to combat any pause that would let death conquer their morale. If one of them fell with pain he was tenderly lifted and treated, but strangling tears must not stop the salutary delirium. It was even encouraged."

Diana and her friends resorted to drugs and alcohol to dull the emotional and physical pain of the war. She developed a taste for chloroform and morphine, which Moore is said to have supplied. "Wine helped and there was wine in plenty—it was said too much," wrote Diana. "George Moore's dances of death flowed with the stuff. They became more frequent as leave became regular from the training centres and the trenches of France and the Middle East." As macabre and surreal as these dances of death were, Diana lived for them. They were a respite from her work at the hospital and the dreary atmosphere at home. Moore's townhouse "became a shelter and a playground for our diminishing Coterie," she wrote.

Diana's male admirers did not like to see her flirting with Moore. She assured them that, despite her outward friendliness, she loathed him. She described the misery of dancing with him, having him "murmur love or Chichtechicher-chich-chich hotly in my ear as we shuffled and bunny-hugged around." In a letter to Raymond Asquith, she described his advances as a "vile torrent of gravy and steaming putrefying blood." After the one alleged occasion when he tried to kiss her—perhaps on that rumored night in her bedroom?—she wrote, "O Raymond, it was so sullying, almost mutilating and scarring."

Are we to believe that Diana's feelings were unequivocally negative? Many accounts of Moore's pursuit of Diana depict him as an overbearing beast preying on a fragile beauty. It's a compelling image, one that fits conveniently into Catherine Bailey's narrative of an innocent young woman being pimped by her heartless mother in order to save the family fortune. No doubt Diana was repelled by Moore's advances; he was nearly twice her age and not endowed with classical good looks.

It's also possible that Diana's horror at Moore's physicality reflected a more general aversion to intimacy. Jamie Charteris, my host at Stanway House, who was related to Diana by marriage, told me confidently that she had always hated sex. "She was too beautiful for that," he said, adding that Diana never minded that her eventual husband, Alfred Duff Cooper, was an incorrigible philanderer because his affairs provided him sexual satisfaction away from her bedroom. As if to prove his point, he added, "Duff cheated on her during their honeymoon!"

But there were many things about the brash American millionaire that appealed to Diana: his sophisticated American tastes, his love of luxury, his generosity. Diana's memoir suggests that she had fond feelings for him. She described him as a "wise man" and "the most loyal and selfless worker in the Allied cause." Looking back on her earlier experiences with him, she wrote, "he had no snobbery. I would have liked him a lot had it not been for his infatuation for me, which frightened me into flight."

Ultimately, it was not Moore's machinations that saved John Manners from risking his life in combat. But that was not for want of trying. He devoted the same degree of effort when the duchess asked for his assistance in an endeavor that involved Diana. In 1915, Diana told her mother that she wanted to leave her position at Guy's Hospital to care for wounded soldiers in Europe. Not surprisingly, the duchess initially refused to let her go. But sensing her daughter's determination, she asked Moore to help set up a hospital in France where Diana could work. She felt that Diana would be safer there than in a makeshift clinic near the battlefront. As Diana recalled in her memoir, Moore "played a big part in this scheme." He commandeered a chateau only thirty-three miles from St. Omer, hired an American director and a staff of nurses and doctors, and gave several thousand pounds for alterations and equipment. He sought additional contributions from several of his rich American friends, including Gordon Selfridge, founder of the Oxford Street department store.

In late summer, just as the hospital was ready to receive patients, the whole plan fell apart. For some reason, the Red Cross had refused to sanction the unit. "I cannot remember how or exactly why, but there was something sinister, I know," wrote Diana. "Was it our backing by the suspect George Moore? Was it my name that was beginning to be overloaded with publicity? Impossible to remember the alleged reasons, but collapse it did."

World War I provided Moore with more opportunities for intrigue on other fronts. As much as he adored Diana, his devotion to Sir John was even stronger. When Moore believed that the general was being treated unfairly by the War Office, he jumped into the fray. With his uncanny ability to engage influential players, he set in motion a chain of events that turned the course of the war.

— CHAPTER 14 —

A Fog of Ignorance and Doubt

IN PRESENT-DAY AMERICA, when news from distant battlefields is available 24/7 on cable television and the Internet, it's hard to imagine a time when the press was not embedded with soldiers in combat all over the world. But war reporting in the heroic style of Ernest Hemingway began with the Spanish-American War in 1898, when publishing titans Joseph Pulitzer and William Randolph Hearst were fighting their own battle for control of the burgeoning newspaper industry. Vying for readers, they sent reporters to Cuba to write sensationalistic stories about Spain's harsh treatment of Cuba and the bravery of Teddy Roosevelt and the Rough Riders. These reports were intended to whip up American animosity toward Spain and promote public support for a war that would be certain to drive up newspaper circulation. The eyewitness coverage stoked America's appetite for fast-breaking news of combat and homegrown heroism. The power of the press to influence national policy was undeniable; when Hearst sent the illustrator and artist Frederick Remington to Cuba with a team of reporters, he told him, "You give me the pictures, I'll give you the war."

George Moore had come of age in the 1890s reading exhilarating accounts of the Spanish-American war by celebrity correspondents like Richard Harding Davis and Stephen Crane. As a newly minted American citizen when the United States joined the war against Spain, he took it for granted that newspapers carried stories reported directly from the battlefield. When World War I broke out, he was astonished that the press was not there to bear witness.

Lord Kitchener had harbored anti-press sentiments since the Boer War, when he felt that journalists had treated him unfairly. Still smarting from that perceived injustice, he banned reporters from the front, claiming that widespread censorship was necessary to protect sensitive military information. The shreds of information passed by the censors lacked specificity and color. In the absence of firsthand reporting, the British public had only the dimmest notion of their soldiers' actions on the battlefield. Moore knew that Germany had taken a very different tack, urging its press and neutral journalists to cover the exploits of its vaunted army. This approach gave the German government powerful propaganda to shower on its people, rousing support for its imperialist war.

Sir John French had never paid much attention to the press. Five months into the war, he was too busy at the front to worry about the press blackout in England. Moore, on the other hand, had always maintained a close relationship with journalists. He recognized the power of publicity to swing popular opinion and saw the British press embargo as an ill-conceived, paternalistic gesture to keep disturbing news from the public. He believed that lively news reporting from the front would complement rather than compromise the Allied war effort.

Moore also had a strong personal interest in the cause. He believed that Sir John was one of England's greatest military leaders and that he would be unfairly vilified if the true story of the British army's achievements under his command was kept from the public. Under these circumstances, Valentine Williams observed, Moore's "first instinct—the natural American instinct—was to start a newspaper campaign."

Moore had a forceful ally in the press magnate Alfred Charles William Harmsworth, better known as Lord

Northcliffe. A pioneer of tabloid journalism, Northcliffe was a self-made man of Irish origins, much like Moore. Inspired by the rising tide of tabloid dailies in the United States, Northcliffe bought the *London Evening News* in 1894. He started the *Daily Mail* in 1903 and five years later added the *Times* to his portfolio of newspapers. With popular new features such as gossip columns and serialized fiction, he boosted readership enormously; by the time war broke out in 1914, he controlled half the newspaper circulation of London.

Alfred Charles William Harmsworth, Lord Northcliffe, c. 1917

Northcliffe had a strong hand in popular as well as political opinion. As one observer put it, he controlled "the masses and the classes." Some statesmen and military leaders sought his counsel; others reviled him. Like my grandfather, he was fiercely anti-German. Indeed, the Germans so feared his powerful propaganda that in February 1917 they sent a warship to shell his country home in Kent. They missed Northcliffe but killed his gardener's wife. Some of Northcliffe's detractors charged that his anti-German sentiment had fomented war fever in England much as the Hearst and Pulitzer newspapers had in the run-up to the Spanish-American War. He was accused of greed and a thirst for sensationalism. No doubt his objectives were mixed; his news empire needed eyewitness war reporting the way fire needs air. But he was also patriotic and fiercely protective of the soldiers whose lives were in danger, including some of his most beloved relatives.

An editorial by Robert Blatchford in the August 25, 1914, *Daily Mail* entitled "Do You Understand?" urged the British government to "have the courage to tell the British people the truth." The piece conceded that some censorship was needed to protect military secrets but argued that the news blockade was dampening public enthusiasm for the army and hampering the recruitment of volunteer soldiers.

In November 1914, on the heels of the hard-won British victory in the first battle of Ypres, Moore had encountered a despondent Will Irwin at the port in Calais. The reporter told Moore that he had reached Ypres but was sent away by a British officer before he could see any action. He asked Moore for details about the battle, but Moore kept mum. Shortly after meeting Moore in Calais, with no end to the press ban in sight, Irwin had returned to New York.

Moore had a plan. He was ready to help Irwin get the story if Irwin would agree to write it. In January 1915, he sent Irwin a cablegram urging him to return to England so that Moore could help him gain access to the war and "see things." His hopes stoked, Irwin sailed for England once again. He had no idea what lay in store for him when he accepted an invitation to dine at Lancaster Gate. Over dinner, Moore told Irwin that the press blackout was hurting the Allied cause. Irwin needed no persuasion on that score. He too was appalled at the bland, cursory accounts of the war published in British newspapers. "Not a word of 'atmosphere,' description, episode; with rare exceptions not one of those 'hero stories' which do so much to bolster civilian morale," he later wrote. Before the two men parted for the night, Moore revealed his scheme to publish an account of the British victory at Ypres.

Irwin soon learned from Moore and from unbiased observers—including American diplomats, army officers, and fellow newspapermen—the extraordinary truth about the battle at Ypres. Irwin was awestruck by the reports of how the British had held their line against the Germans for three weeks, despite the Germans' larger and better equipped army. He painted a picture of staunch resolution in the face of unrelenting German bombardment. "For numbers engaged, for casualties, this was the greatest battle ever fought by a British army," he later wrote. "Three months had passed; and the British public did not yet know all this!"

Irwin conceived of the story as an American newspaper scoop. But Moore had grander hopes for it. In early 1915 he had called on Lord Northcliffe, telling the publisher everything he knew about the War Office's refusal to produce the high explosive shells that Sir John had demanded. The two men agreed that only if the British public knew what was really happening on the front would the War Office be pressured into taking action. Moore believed that news of the heroic battle at Ypres would move the British people to insist that the army be supplied with adequate weapons.

Moore sent Irwin to meet Lord Northcliffe. When Irwin told him he was writing an account of the Ypres battle, the press lord offered to print Irwin's story in his London newspapers in defiance of the War Office. Northcliffe knew that the War Office would not dare discredit such an account of British heroism. At the same time, knowing that censors would ruin or suppress the story if it were cabled to the *Tribune* in New York, Northcliffe promised to avoid the censors by sending it by courier on the fastest boat to New York.

Moore did everything he could to bring the article to print. He invited Irwin to stay at Lancaster Gate, where he set him up at a desk with a view of French's golden Field Marshal's baton displayed in a gilt case. He provided Irwin with French's firsthand reports of the battle. Moore also brought Northcliffe and one of his military experts to the house to edit Irwin's copy as he drafted it. A week later, on April 6, 1915, the story appeared in the *Times,* the *Daily Mail,* and the *New York Tribune.*

The news accounts of First Ypres triggered widespread jubilation. People on the street recognized Irwin from his photograph in the press and personally thanked him. "Hardened British newspapermen congratulated me with tears in their eyes," he wrote. Arthur Balfour, the former Conservative prime minister who would soon replace Winston Churchill as First Lord of the Admiralty, sent him a note describing the piece as "the greatest battle story in our language." There was such demand for the article that Northcliffe had it specially printed in a penny pamphlet. Four million copies were sold. Irwin became a celebrity overnight, receiving invitations from many of London's social elite, some of whom he had already met at Lancaster Gate. Irwin enjoyed the attention. He noted that, despite the war, the British aristocracy "maintained the ghost of its old habits—informal dinners, offhand luncheons, modest weekend parties. I could have dined out five times a week." He added, "I even became a temporary member of clubs whose doors any outsider seldom darkens."

In late March 1915, as Will Irwin's article about Ypres was being rushed into print in London, hostilities were beginning anew in France. The lack of sufficient ammunition—high explosive shells, in particular—was keenly felt in the Battle of Neuve Chappelle, where British forces attacked the German line on a low-lying, swampy plain in northwestern France. The British succeeded in breaking through the German line but were unable to exploit this advantage because they had run out of ammunition. A British colonel who had witnessed the carnage at Neuve Chappelle remarked that the Germans were "holding the line with machinery, we with lives."

Kitchener, still unwilling to acknowledge the ammunition shortage, argued that the commander-in-chief's incompetence had brought about the stalemate at Neuve Chappelle. He lambasted French for his "recklessly extravagant" use of shells in the battle. Moore was outraged that Kitchener should blame French for his army's failure. "No matter what his past had been," he wrote in his memoir, "Lord Kitchener never realized the demands of modern war and the need of modern explosives."

Galvanized by the success of Will Irwin's article and furious at the War Office's continuing obstinacy, Moore was determined to publicize what he felt was the truth about Neuve Chappelle. He had someone in mind for the job. Moore had first met Valentine Williams in February 1915, a month before the fatal explosion at Helfaut that they both had witnessed. Moore knew that Williams was a regular guest of his friend Lady Maud Cunard, and he asked her to introduce them. Happy to oblige, she invited both men to lunch. Williams had expected to meet the Irish writer George Moore, for whom Lady Maud had long served as a muse and confidante. Instead, he was surprised to find himself "shaking hands with a burly . . . Californian, who, I discovered, shared a house at 94 Lancaster Gate with Sir John French."

Once Williams had figured out which George Moore he was dining with, the two men fell into a discussion about the press ban. Moore immediately made clear his opposition to it. He knew that a gripping battle story by a veteran reporter like Williams would seriously undermine the legitimacy of the press ban. Moore arranged for Williams to meet with Sir John, who happened to be in London for a few days. The general got right to the point, telling Williams that he had believed all along that the press ban was a mistake and that he was in London to bring the policy to an end. Sir John assured the correspondent that he would be allowed visit the front. Several days later, at Sir John's invitation, Williams brought his boss, Lord Northcliffe, to 94 Lancaster Gate. Northcliffe followed up the meeting by sending Sir John a letter expressing his hope that he would soon have the munitions he needed to prevail against the Germans. The press lord began to make frequent visits to GHQ, joining the effort to demand high explosive shells for the British troops.

True to his word, French summoned Williams to GHQ on March 26. The correspondent was given a seat in the commander-in-chief's dining hall and a bed in the quarters of the aides-de-camp across the road from French's house. With the British army's failure to prevail at Neuve Chappelle still stinging at GHQ, French was eager to have Williams write a piece detailing how the battle had unfolded. He gave Williams General Douglas Haig's confidential report on the battle and told him to go wherever he wanted. A private car would be at his disposal. Williams called this "war corresponding de luxe."

Armed with a sealed letter of introduction from Haig's chief of intelligence, Williams visited commanders of all the brigades that had taken part in the battle, but they refused to give him any useful information. He was puzzled by their response until one general, a Scots Guardsman known as Pa Heyworth, revealed to him the contents of Haig's letter. It ordered that no confidential documents be disclosed to the reporter, "but merely material for what the writer, with a nice command of Fleet Street jargon, described as a 'human interest story.'" As Williams recalled, Heyworth "uttered a snort of contempt and said, 'You'd better read the Brigade diary. It's confidential, but that's your funeral! There you are!' And he slapped it down in front of me."

Williams proceeded to visit the units detailed in the Brigade diary and got firsthand accounts of the battle. From the roof of a half-ruined farmhouse near Neuve Chappelle, he surveyed the German trenches. He understood that he could not criticize the British army's tactics or speculate on the sufficiency of its weapons; he had been directed to write a straightforward account of how the battle had been fought. But he concluded privately that the shortage of ammunition was to blame for the ultimate failure of the attack. He drafted his article and gave it to Northcliffe, who had come to GHQ at French's invitation. The piece was read and approved by French, his director of military intelligence, and Northcliffe himself.

Although Northcliffe had originally intended to publish Williams's article only in the *Daily Mail,* at the last minute he decided to distribute it to all newspapers through the London Press Bureau. That way, he figured, his competitors would not feel they had been scooped and would be more likely to support his cause. The story was published anonymously in all the morning papers on April 19, 1915.

Like Will Irwin's article two weeks earlier, Williams's piece was a nationwide sensation. Walter Long, a member of the House of Commons, said, "I do not believe that anyone who read that story could fail to feel that it would have the most wonderful effect on the people and that this was the kind of account for which we have so long and often asked." Lord Derby, an influential politician and military figure, also weighed in. "I venture to think that the account brought in more recruits than the speech of any minister or ex-minister," he wrote. "People like to see described in other than purely official language what regiments have done." General French himself sent Williams a letter thanking him for the piece. "It is *excellent* and exactly what we wanted," he wrote. "You have done the army a good service."

Newspapers also praised the article. An editorial in the *Pall Mall Gazette* declared that "the veil that has been lifted by so brilliant a piece of journalism must not again be allowed to fall between the nation and those who are fighting and dying on its behalf."

The publication of the two blockbuster articles had put a dent in the press ban. The British people were hungry for news, and their support for the war grew as they learned what their soldiers were up against. During the spring of 1915 the War Office had grudgingly begun to send reporters on special tours. By June the press could come and go freely—though, of course, reports were censored to protect sensitive information. But the sensational pieces didn't bring immediate relief in the form of better ammunition for the troops. The weapons shortage continued to worsen, exacerbated by the Allies' decision to extend the fighting to the Dardanelles. In March, the War Office had informed French that ammunition he had requested was being rerouted to fight the Turks on the Eastern front. French and his officers resented the shift in strategy, dismissing the battles in the East as "ridiculous little side-shows."

French's spirits sank even lower when Prime Minister Asquith gave a speech at Newcastle on April 20, 1915, asserting that he had consulted with Kitchener and was confident that the British army had all the ammunition it required. Asquith dismissed the suggestion that the government's failure to provide adequate ammunition was crippling the war effort. Not only is it untrue, he said, but it could only dishearten Britain's troops and allies while encouraging the Germans. French was devastated. "When I read this speech," he wrote, "after all my public and private appeals, I lost any hope that I had entertained of receiving help from the Government as then constituted."

Moore and Northcliffe were determined to press the cause further. After Asquith's speech, Northcliffe suggested in a letter to French that he make "a short and very vigorous statement . . . to a private correspondent (the usual way of making things public in England) . . . that would tell the people here the truth and thus bring public pressure on the Government to stop men and munitions pouring away to the Dardanelles, as they are at present." The idea stuck in French's mind. On May 9, 1915, the British engaged the Germans again in the area of Neuve Chappelle in a two-day conflict at Aubers Ridge. Sir John was apprehensive. Soon after the battle began, Kitchener informed him that 20 percent of his ammunition reserve had been redirected to the Dardanelles.

As French had feared, the Battle of Aubers Ridge was catastrophic. The Germans had substantially reinforced their barbed-wire defenses since Neuve Chappelle, and the shells of the British army were too light, and fired from worn-out guns, to make any crack in the German line. One frustrated officer wrote, "Our attack has failed, and failed badly, and with heavy casualties. That is the bald and more unpleasant fact." He blamed the War Office for the debacle. "No one is to blame—at least no one in France. It is deplorable that a great country like England cannot keep the small army we have here, even now, supplied with ammunition."

Sir John and Moore observed the battle from the tower of a demolished church. Sir John later recalled, "as I watched the Aubers Ridge, I clearly saw the great inequality of the artillery duels, and, as attack after attack failed, I could see that the absence of sufficient artillery support was doubling and trebling our losses in men." He told Moore that he was going to take drastic measures even if he risked his position in doing so. He had previously spoken to the press about the need for more high explosive shells but had stopped short of blaming the ammunition shortage for the loss of British soldiers' lives. This was about to change.

That same day, another of Northcliffe's war correspondents, Charles à Court Repington, arrived at GHQ, at Moore and Northcliffe's invitation. Repington was a controversial figure. Like Sir John French, he was an incorrigible womanizer. He had joined the British Rifle Brigade in 1878, and by 1902 he had reached the position of colonel. But he was forced to resign when it became known that he was having an affair with the wife of a British official in Egypt. An outspoken advocate for a strong British military, he was impetuous and indiscreet, qualities that suited him perfectly for the task Moore and Northcliffe had in mind for him. They wanted him to hear directly from Sir John about the ammunition shortage. They knew he would jump at the chance to reveal how the lack of ammunition was hobbling the British army and taking the lives of its soldiers.

The events that soon unfolded came to be known as the Shells Scandal, a critical turning point in the war. That night, French gave Repington all his past correspondence with the War Office regarding the army's need for more and better armaments. With those materials in hand, Repington began drafting an article. At Moore's insistence, French also sent two top staff members to London armed with copies of the correspondence and a memorandum that thoroughly detailed the problem. Within days, French's emissaries were meeting with Conservative Party leaders and with David Lloyd George, then Chancellor of the Exchequer, who had openly criticized the government's handling of the war.

Repington's article, headlined "NEED FOR SHELLS: BRITISH ATTACK CHECKED: LIMITED SUPPLIES THE CAUSE," appeared in the *Times* on May 14. His assertion that "the want of an unlimited supply of high explosive shells was a fatal bar to our success" squarely contradicted Prime Minister Asquith's pronouncement at Newcastle three weeks earlier that the army had sufficient ammunition.

As Moore and Northcliffe anticipated, the article generated widespread public outrage over the government's failure to supply its troops adequately. The Shells Scandal, coupled with bad news from the Dardanelles, forced Prime Minister Asquith to dismantle his all-liberal government and replace it with a coalition government. The Ministry of Munitions was created, with David Lloyd George in charge, a development that sharply limited Kitchener's power as Secretary of War.

The Shells Scandal had an immediate impact on the British war effort. By June, England was fully engaged in ammunition production, with large numbers of women going to work in arms factories. Winston Churchill and Lloyd George appeared publicly to declare that supporting the war effort was the "absolute duty of every citizen." And the scandal brought a final end to the press ban. In an article that summer for the American monthly magazine *Metropolitan*, Will Irwin declared that the scandal was the "real climax" of the war for Great Britain. "Outwardly the War Office led the newspapers along, holding out unfilled promises for next week or next month," he wrote. "Inwardly, Kitchener was standing off certain members of the cabinet who begged him to send reporters to the lines." Meanwhile, he continued, "the British people, ravenous for news, were getting little nibbles at the rind of truth. Until May, the British press never hinted at a shortage of high explosive shells."

Repington's bombshell had everyone speculating as to who had initiated the leak of information. While French claimed years later that it was *his* idea to take action, no one believed him. Valentine Williams unequivocally named Moore as the instigator. Political leaders also pointed to Moore. French's secretary, Brinsley Fitzgerald, wrote to a friend that Moore was "a curious fellow. . . . He is a mad enthusiast about French, and equally mad in his bitterness against Kitchener, and being an American wouldn't have the same ideas about the Press as you or I have."

In his memoir, Moore ultimately claimed credit for the Repington exposé. He wrote, "We were compelled to have Col. Repington, after the Battle of Aubers Ridge in an article which appeared in the LONDON TIMES, say in effect, that the lack of high explosives and shells . . . was a fatal bar to the Army's success."

— CHAPTER 15 —

A German Spy at GHQ?

MOORE'S INVOLVEMENT WITH THE PRESS did not end with the Shells Scandal. A few weeks later, a man with the unwieldy name of West Fenton de Wend-Fenton, editor and proprietor of the popular society magazine *London Weekly World,* wrote a column suggesting that Moore was up to no good:

> Many questions have been asked as to the constant journeyings between London and British headquarters of an American citizen named Mr. George Moore, who has no official standing either in the British Army or in any of its subsidiary forces, such as the Red Cross Society, and who is apparently a financier of uncertain standing whose chief claim to recognition seems to be in his acquisition of the interests of a Mr. Lowenfeld, an unnaturalized German, in a concern known as the Investment Registry. This person is understood to be on terms of the closest intimacy with Sir John French.
>
> Mr. Moore, in his frequent visits to London, is said to make very outspoken comments on the inner happenings both at

home and abroad, and on the face of it, it seems extremely undesirable that a private citizen of a neutral country should be afforded such exceptional facilities for knowing the innermost secrets of the campaign.

In early June 1915, Moore announced his plan to return to New York. De Wend-Fenton coyly claimed responsibility for this. "In June," he wrote, "Mr. Moore received a polite intimation that a change of air might be beneficial to his health and he took his departure for America. I . . . rejoiced to think that I might have been the humble instrument of removing an extremely dangerous personage from the war zone." Denying that his departure was in any way connected with the recent flurry of negative publicity, Moore insisted that he had important business to attend to at home. He sailed from Liverpool aboard the SS *New York* on June 12. His departure was reported in the *Washington Herald* under the headline "Liner Braves Submarines."

Moore's peculiar role at the front also drew criticism in the American press. On July 4, 1915, an anonymous "veteran diplomat" wrote a column in the *New York Times Magazine* lamenting Sir John's association with the mysterious American millionaire. "French became entangled about four years ago in the toils of one of the fastest crowds of titled people in London," wrote the disgruntled diplomat. "Then, two years ago he developed that much-discussed intimacy with his great American crony and friend, George Gordon Moore of Detroit, Michigan and of England." The anonymous columnist went on to complain that Moore has been "an almost constant guest" of the Field Marshal at GHQ in France since the beginning of the war. "There Moore has been accorded privileges and prerogatives denied to all British visitors, even to members of the Government administration, and to peers of the realm, as well as to distinguished Frenchmen of official rank," he wrote.

SIR JOHN FRENCH'S FRIEND

George Gordon Moore of Detroit, whose intimacy with Sir John French has enabled him to be near the firing line since the British expeditionary force went to France and whose presence there has been resented by some of the public men of England, perhaps is least known among those of his own community. And what is more, he never has made an effort to attract public attention, although his operations have been among the most extensive in America in the last decade.

He merged the interests of urban and interurban lines and built up the Michigan United Traction company, with 350 miles of track, then sold it to an eastern corporation, incidentally making millions for himself. Several years ago he organized a $50,000,000 water power corporation in Georgia, and later he amalgamated the Pacific coast utilities. He also heads a great corporation with extensive interests in Brazil.

He is a man of tremendous nervous energy and seems never to tire, although he now has very widespread interests. In the Canadian Northwest he has a vast cattle range; he controls the traction company at Lincoln, Neb., a water power in Texas and another in Vermont.

Although he has been tremendously busy he has found time for recreation, and is a sportsman with many fancies. He plays polo, tennis and other outdoor games, and is an expert rifle shot.

The friendship between Mr. Moore and Sir John French is of several years' standing. Always they were together when in London, and a couple of years ago when the Balkan troubles threatened to cause international difficulties he was with the field marshal day and night.

Chicago Eagle, July 17, 1915

The most vicious attack on Moore was published in *The Vital Issue*, a pro-German newspaper based in New York. Titled "The New Achille and his Patrocles, Sir John French and George Gordon Moore," the piece hinted heavily that the men were romantically involved. Accompanying the piece was a cartoon depicting Moore as an effeminate dandy and French as a virile military hero. "It was difficult to imagine such a man," the piece read, "with his soft voice, his white hands, his almost chubby face, and even, white teeth, spending almost all his time near scenes of war and exerting no small influence in the conduct of the British campaign."

As further proof of Moore and French's alleged illicit relationship, the writer noted their communal living arrangement. "It seems strange also that Mr. Moore and Sir John French until the war began should have lived together in a large house at Lancaster Gate," he wrote. "They were so inseparable that the American has been with the English general almost constantly at the front." Moore shrugged off the suggestion of impropriety, saying, "Yes, Sir John French and I live together. I see nothing strange in that. I think a great deal of him and I hope the feeling is mutual."

THE VITAL ISSUE 13

The New Achille and His Patrocles.

Sir John French and George Gordon Moore.

(Compiled from the New York "Sun" and "World")

"George Gordon Moore, the American traction man whose intimacy with Sir John French, the British commander, has gained him a freedom at the British headquarters 'somewhere in France' *that is causing criticism and wonderment in England,* has come to this country to look after his extensive interests in and about Detroit, Mich.

"At the Hotel Manhattan yesterday Mr. Moore denied that his leaving the Continent was concerned with recent articles in London and New York newspapers intimating that Sir John French was showing his *American friend too great consideration.* * * *"

* * * * *

"Mr. Moore looks almost anything but the remarkably successful business man, lawyer and promoter that he is. One gets the impression of an Englishman living on his income rather than of a man who two years ago, at the age of 37, had so successfully managed many American corporations that he could retire from active business. * * *"

* * * * *

"This man who is so close to the great British field commander is below middle height, *quiet of manner and with a soft, almost lisping voice, and possessed of a most contagious and omnipresent smile. His is the face of a man rather fond of the good things of life,* not one who is the bosom friend of the general commanding nobody knows how many hundreds of thousands of fighting men.

"It was difficult to imagine such a man, *with his soft voice, his white hands, his almost chubby face,* and even, *white teeth,* spending almost all his time near scenes of war and *exerting no small influence in the conduct of the British campaign. It seems strange* also that Mr. Moore and Sir John French until the war began should have lived together in a large house *at Lancaster Gate, overlooking Kensington Gardens. They were so inseparable* that the American has been with the English general almost constantly at the front. Mr. Moore explains it in this wise:

"'Yes, Sir John French and I live together. *I see nothing strange in that. I think a great deal of him and I hope the feeling is mutual.* * * *"

"* * * * *and he smiled his appealing smile.*

* * * * *

"Mr. Moore smiled that smile several times during his conversation, but for all his smiles it was evident that the thought of an interview was not pleasant. 'Now, just see what I have got into,' he remarked— *again smiling*—to one of a *little group of tastefully dressed young men who surround him,* when the reporter made known his errand. * * *"

* * * * *

"* * * *As to the stories that a good many ladies have been entertained at headquarters, I know of only*

Seemingly impervious to these attacks, Moore threw his energy into drumming up public support for entering the war. His unique position at British GHQ made him an instant celebrity. Newspapers described him as "the most interviewed man today in America." Seizing the moment, he asserted that the Germans were determined to conquer Europe and press on to America. He urged the United States to shake off its complacency and join the Allied cause before it was too late. In an interview with the *Detroit Free Press*, he recounted the horrors of the Germans' chlorine gas attack several months earlier. "Our people ought to see the victims," he said. "Burning at the stake is humane by comparison. It only shows what this country would have to face if there were war. It is a sign to get ready." To bolster his arguments, Moore was not above fomenting virulent propaganda. He accused German soldiers of crucifying young Canadian officers. "They have nailed them to village crosses," he said, adding that the German army's cruelties "would make any of our Indian wars of bygone days look like a condition of Utopian peace." He described German civilization as "a veneer which covers the basest and most brutal passions imaginable." The *Detroit Free Press* interview went viral, appearing in newspapers on both sides of the Atlantic. The Allies were thrilled.

Moore took other opportunities to whip Americans into war frenzy. At the annual VFW convention in Detroit in August 1915, he gave a speech titled "The German Menace." He began by lambasting the United States government for letting its military fall into "a deplorable state of unpreparedness." But then he went much further, claiming that the Germans had already infiltrated the United States. He told the audience that two and a half million German-American reservists, not naturalized and subject to the Kaiser's order, regularly reported to German and Austrian consulates across the country and stood ready to attack America. Moore warned that "within 48 hours, on an order from the Kaiser, a division of these soldiers could be marched down Woodward

Avenue singing 'Deutschland Uber Alles' and marching with their famous goose-step."

This charge drew vehement objections and denials from the German-American community and elsewhere. Moore received several death threats after giving the talk. Even the *Detroit Free Press*, which had long been one of Moore's staunchest champions, demanded that he produce proof of his damning accusations. Having no such evidence, Moore waffled in his response, proposing that the German ambassador should offer, as Germany's "evidence of good faith and friendship" a detailed enumeration of the number of German-trained troops and the amount of German ammunition currently in the United States. The newspaper dismissed this suggestion as rude and impracticable. Moore's sensational allegations caught the attention of Robert Lansing, the newly appointed Secretary of State, who alerted the Attorney General with a brief note: "I have the honor to enclose, for your information and for such action as you deem it deserves, the Sunday morning, August 29, 1915, edition of the SYRACUSE HERALD, containing a press dispatch from Detroit reporting a speech made in that city by Mr. George Gordon Moore alleging that Germany has a large reservist army in the United States already organized and provided with large stores of ammunition." Evidently the Attorney General was not convinced of the danger.

On December 4, 1915, Moore learned that Prime Minister Lloyd George had demanded French's resignation. He was not entirely surprised by this news. Over the past several months, the commander-in-chief had come under heavy criticism from all sides. In September, he had been held responsible for a personnel snafu that led to the Allied defeat at the Battle of Loos. In November, French was assailed in the House of Lords for late-night parties and the unexplained presence of ladies at GHQ. As winter approached, the war was widely perceived to have reached a stalemate under French's leadership.

On December 5, with great reluctance, French resigned. After a couple of weeks of painful good-byes, he sailed for home. As he made his way to Boulogne, thousands of troops lined the road for miles to bid him farewell. While many criticized French's strategic skills, no one doubted his concern for the rank-and-file soldiers. Sir William Robertson, the first British soldier to rise from the rank of private to field marshal, did not always agree with French, but he praised his commitment to his soldiers. "Sir John was exceedingly popular with the troops," he wrote, "and I doubt if any other general in the army could have sustained in them to the same extent the courage and resolution which they displayed during the trying circumstances of the first six months of the war." As French walked up the gangplank, the 19th Hussars, a British cavalry troop quartered nearby, surrounded him, cheering him until they were hoarse.

Upon hearing the news of French's resignation, Moore immediately sailed for England. Annoyed that Moore had dared return to London, de Wend-Fenton decided it was time to take the gloves off. He had already questioned Moore's bona fides, insinuating a dubious business relationship with a German financier. But in his January 26, 1916, editorial in the *London Weekly World* he went further, strongly suggesting that Moore had been passing British military secrets to the Germans. Moore's recent sojourn in America had provided de Wend-Fenton with what he believed was the smoking gun in the supposed espionage plot. "It is interesting to note," he wrote, "that, within a few days after his arrival in America [in June 1915] he is said to have been a guest at a Long Island house where Count von Bernstorff, the German Ambassador, also was staying." He added that "a lady understood to be his sister, Miss Moore, is known to be an intimate friend of von Bernstorff." While concluding that "Moore may be a perfectly harmless citizen," he insisted that Moore's "association with Lord French is invidious and in the interest of the General, no less than of the country, should be terminated, or at least postponed, until the war is over."

Moore sued the newspaper for libel. The lawsuit made headlines in all the major American newspapers, including the *Boston Globe,* which reported that "the trial promises to be most sensational." On March 9, 1916, the trial took place in a crowded courtroom. Moore testified that his only visit to Long Island had been to the home of his friend Theodore Roosevelt, and that his only living sister was an elderly invalid living in Canada, and that she had never met Count Von Bernstorff.

Sir John French took the stand on Moore's behalf, attesting to his close personal relationship with Moore and the reason for Moore's presence at GHQ starting in the autumn of 1914. After French testified that Moore's services at the front were "invaluable" and that he had "absolute confidence" in Moore's integrity, the judge promptly declared the charges against Moore to be "infamous and wholly unfounded." Shortly afterwards, the triumphant Moore sailed again for New York.

The gossip surrounding Moore's alleged German espionage did not die with the successful conclusion of his libel trial. Like the suggestion that he had "Red Indian" blood on account of his jet-black hair, prominent nose, and ruddy complexion, the rumor about Moore spying for the Germans was woven into his shadowy past. Another widespread story was that Moore was the son of King Edward VII, the adulterous "playboy prince," and was banished to America as a remittance man with a hefty allowance to keep him quiet. There were also suggestions of violence in Moore's past, which

Moore himself might have fomented. According to Tommy Hitchcock's son Billy, Moore had told his father that "if he ever needed to have someone killed, Moore was the person he should call." Similar tales floated among Gatsby's guests, who whispered that their host was "a German spy during the war," "a nephew or a cousin of Kaiser Wilhelm's," and that he had "killed a man who had found out that he was nephew to Von Hindenburg."

Moore's shadowy business dealings, like Gatsby's, caused people to wonder about the source of his seemingly endless supply of money. Moore often ran off to California or Canada to placate anxious investors and patch up quasi-legal business arrangements. As with Gatsby, some people assumed Moore was a bootlegger. Others claimed that he had been run out of England after it was discovered that he had sold worthless securities to dozens of prominent British investors. As it turned out, there was truth behind this surreptitious gossip.

Like Gatsby, Moore was a tantalizing enigma. No one knew much about his past, and he seemed to like it that way. Throughout his life, rumors had followed him like a hungry dog. People thronged to his parties not only because of his grand hospitality, but because it was titillating to imagine that their host was part "Red Indian," or a bastard son of royalty, or a swindler, just as Gatsby's party guests experienced a frisson of excitement gossiping about their host's dark secrets. I think Moore enjoyed the speculation about his past and the mystery of his money; it heightened his allure.

— CHAPTER 16 —

"I Always Fear What Too Many Know"

MOORE'S VICTORY IN THE LIBEL TRIAL did more than clear his name of the espionage charge. After years of gossip in the newspapers and elsewhere about Moore's relationship with Sir John French, the trial had given Sir John the opportunity to publicly declare his admiration for and trust in his American friend. When Moore returned to the United States in the spring of 1916, his ties to Sir John opened doors to the country's political elite.

One of the first people Moore befriended in the spring of 1916 was Edward M. House, President Wilson's chief advisor on European politics and diplomacy. Although House had no official title, he was arguably the most powerful man in the president's inner circle. His unquestioned authority had earned him the courtesy title of "colonel" despite his lack of military service. Colonel House chose to live in New York rather than Washington, D.C., and conducted business from a small study in his home. Moore met Colonel House through a mutual friend named Florence Jaffray Harriman, a Washington socialite with extensive political ties. (Harriman was one of the hardy souls who had visited Moore's hunting preserve on Hooper Bald. In a note to House dated November 28, 1916, she described the trip as "a most strenuous and delightful ten days" and proudly announced that her companion had shot a bear.)

"Colonel" Edward M. House, 1920

House lived just down the block from Moore, and the two men saw each other often. House knew that Moore had spent much of the previous decade in England and that he had many reliable contacts there, including Sir John French. Moore and House often discussed their shared belief that the United States should enter the war, and Moore offered to help make this happen in any way possible. "From that time until the end of the war," wrote Moore, "I was almost in daily contact with him, and because of my frequent trips to England, I kept him posted on the 'low-down.'"

In January 1917, several months before the United States entered the war, House sent Moore to England to assess the growing severity of the country's food shortage. Moore had made the risky transatlantic journey several times since the war started, as if thumbing his nose at the Germans. On one trip, a fire in the ship's hold had precipitated a dangerous three-day run into New York Harbor. But this latest crossing on the SS *Philadelphia* was even more hair-raising.

On January 31, 1917, Germany announced its "sink on sight" policy, threatening all ships in the Atlantic Ocean. New York Harbor was immediately put under embargo, but it was too late for the *Philadelphia*, which had departed New York five days earlier. Life went on in the same luxurious manner—first-class passengers dressed in evening clothes for sumptuous dinners—but the mood was anything but festive. Everyone worried that a torpedo might strike at any moment. Midway through the trip an explosive sound erupted from the ship's engines, sending the passengers into a panic. It turned out that the terrible noise had been caused by the rupture of one of the ship's crankshafts. This was less grave than a German torpedo but the passengers had much to fear, since the rupture had taken out the ship's right engine. As the *New York Herald* reported, the *Philadelphia* made the remainder of the crossing "at a snail's pace through the very midst of the danger zone marked out for the operations of the latest phase of Prussian frightfulness."

The ship arrived in Liverpool two days late, but unharmed, and Moore proceeded to London on his fact-finding mission. "I was in England four days," he wrote. "I arrived on Monday and on Wednesday we had Lloyd George and Winston Churchill to dinner. As a result of this meeting, I secured the information." Moore returned to New York on February 28 and reported to House that if the Germans continued to destroy British ships at the same rate, the country would be facing starvation by December.

America's entry into the war in April of 1917 inspired Moore to launch his own scheme to defeat the Germans. Having sailed through the U-Boat-laced Atlantic waters on several occasions, he understood as well as anyone the threat German submarines posed to American and Allied vessels. Within two weeks of the United States' declaration of war, the Germans had sunk 122 ocean-going ships. In October, Moore presented House with his plan to build a concrete barrier across the North Sea from England to Denmark that would block German ships from interfering with Allied ships in the Atlantic. Moore's audacious proposal was no pipe dream. He had retained a prominent naval architect and two engineering firms specializing in reinforced concrete to design the barrier. Moore estimated the project could be completed in as little as ten months. Moore's idea was approved by experts in anti-submarine warfare and military engineers, including General George Goethals, who supervised the building of the Panama Canal. The estimated cost for the barrier was $254 million. While this seemed an exorbitant sum, Moore pointed out that it was approximately the value of Allied ships destroyed by the Germans every four months.

One of Moore's major concerns was that the British would have a hard time accepting such a gargantuan plan whose results would only be seen after a year or more. In a handwritten letter to House, Moore suggested sending a mission of engineers and industrial leaders to England to introduce the plan to British authorities. Moore urged House to maintain absolute secrecy about the trip to preclude any leak to the Germans, who would attempt to sink the American ship. The note concluded, "If possible, do it with only the knowledge of the President and yourself, and without the Council for Defence. At the moment it might be wisest. I always fear what too many know." The Council of National Defense consisted of the Secretaries of War, the Navy, the Interior, Commerce, Agriculture, and Labor. To organize a mission to England on behalf of the United States without their knowledge would seem a tall order. But Moore thrived on this sort of intrigue.

Many far-fetched military proposals surfaced after the United States entered the war, including a project to plant 100,000 mines across the North Sea. Moore's barrier never got off the drawing board. But his scheme reflected the magnitude of his confidence in American industry and engineering skill to accomplish great things. Surely, he believed, if the United States could build the Panama Canal, it could build a 300-mile barrier across the North Sea.

Once the United States entered the war, Moore did not hesitate to share his views with the Wilson administration about how the war should be conducted. In a memorandum to Colonel House, he expressed his opinion that the secret of the Germans' superiority lay in the organization of their General Staff, which exercised broad supervision over the field commanders and the allocation of their resources, taking the management burden off the commander-in-chief. General John Pershing, Commander-in-Chief of the American Expeditionary Force, organized the structure of the new army along the lines Moore had recommended. Moore also cautioned against sending troops too quickly into battle. In a letter to House dated May 22, 1917, he wrote "I have a vivid memory of the Dardanelles Expedition conceived with the same enthusiasm and lack of sanity and military thought." Moore urged that England and France should cease their futile offensive attacks and instead maintain their lines of defense until the United States could come in with an "overwhelming superiority in men and material" that would break the German lines and defeat its army. Moore knew there would be opposition to this more cautious approach. "I recognize that at the moment this course is unpopular," he wrote, "but the certainty that such forces are coming will be a stimulant to our Allies and a depressing influence upon the Germans, and will avoid the needless wastage of American lives until the time when the sacrifice is warranted." House immediately forwarded Moore's letter to President Wilson, who forwarded it to Newton Diehl Baker, Secretary of War. "The memorandum from George G. Moore about defensive and offensive warfare on the western front in Europe makes a considerable impression on me and I should very much like to discuss it with you," wrote Wilson.

Baker shared Moore's letter with General Tasker Bliss, Assistant Chief of Staff of the Army, who was likewise impressed with Moore's ideas. But despite Bliss's endorsement, Baker rejected Moore's proposal because he believed that Americans would not accept a long period of preparation before going to war. Adopting Moore's view, Bliss rejected the idea of sending American troops who were neither properly trained nor equipped to join the Allies in the trenches. He reasoned that such a scheme would waste American lives without giving the American army any control over how the war was to be fought. "When the war is over it may be a literal fact that the American flag will not have appeared anywhere on the line because our organizations will simply be parts of battalions and regiments of the Entente Allies," he wrote. "We might have a million men there and yet no American army and no American commander. . . . I do not believe our people will stand for it." The strategy urged by Moore and Bliss prevailed. Although a few American soldiers were sent to Europe in June, the full American Expeditionary Forces stayed out of combat until October 1917, when they had the strength to bring about a definitive Allied victory against the Germans.

— CHAPTER 17 —

Reckonings

I DON'T KNOW HOW EARLY IN HIS CAREER my grandfather started running afoul of the law in his business dealings. There were rumblings early on about his failure to repay bank loans and his mishandling of shareholder funds as he built his Michigan railroad empire. He had managed to avoid the consequences of his chicanery, for a time at least, by setting up shop in a new venue, on a different continent. But he couldn't escape the long arm of the law forever. In October 1918 he faced a reckoning on two fronts: one personal, the other professional.

Moore's relations with the Investment Registry had soured since he had taken control of the company in 1910. He had made several investments on behalf of the Registry that were not only self-serving but disastrous financially to the Registry's other investors. A committee of shareholders made an investigation in 1911 and issued a report that officially cleared the company of any impropriety. But among London's financial community, the report was viewed with skepticism. One newspaper called it "farcical." Moore's control of the Registry generated mistrust and suspicion. In 1916, the *Sporting Times* reported that Moore was "persona non grata" at the Registry's offices and suggested that "Mr. Wemyss (Lord Elcho) on the subject of Moore might make interesting reading." But even when it was becoming clear that Moore was a swindler, he managed to remain in the good graces of high society.

In 1917, disgruntled members of the Investment Registry conspired to kick Moore out of the company. By an astonishing coincidence of the sort that befell my grandfather many times, he learned of this scheme in time to thwart it. One of Moore's friends in London was a flamboyant American named Jean Sifton, known in her heyday as the best and most expensively dressed woman in the world. Sifton was having dinner with her husband and some friends one evening when it was mentioned that "a shady business deal was about to be sprung on George Moore." The story Sifton heard was that Moore's associates at the Registry by some nefarious means had managed to sell his holdings, so that they apparently had gained control and were about to throw him out. She alerted Moore first thing the next morning in time for him to thwart the mutiny. In gratitude, Moore told her, "I want you to always remember this: any time you need anything, whatever it is, call on George Moore. Anything I CAN do for you I WILL." Moore made good his promise by giving her legal advice that enabled her to divorce her husband so that she could marry Captain John Nash, an Englishman with whom she had had a long and not very secret affair.

But Moore's legal troubles with the Investment Registry were just beginning. The investment in Whiting Manufacturing had involved building a railroad through the Smoky Mountains and cutting timber to be transported on the railroad. Problems arose in getting the operation up and running, and Investment Registry shareholders were paying large amounts of additional money to Moore every month to fund it. They accused him of diverting money from the railway construction into his own pocket. Moore attempted to transfer ownership of the Investment Registry's shares in Whiting to a dummy corporation that he controlled. On October 2, 1918, the Investment Registry filed a lawsuit against Moore in New York to regain the shares in

Whiting that Moore had, in effect, stolen. The court issued an injunction the same day preventing Moore from doing anything with the shares pending a trial on the merits, which he eventually lost.

Meanwhile, back in Detroit, Moore's wife, Elizabeth, had filed for divorce several months earlier on grounds of "neglect and extreme cruelty." Her primary complaint was that Moore had failed to support her financially. Rubberneckers and reporters crowded the courtroom to watch the trial. Although Elizabeth complained of financial hardship, she appeared for the trial "richly dressed and furred," according to news reports. She was accompanied by her French maid, who testified as her corroborating witness, and her daughter, Virginia, who had come home from boarding school for the occasion. Elizabeth spoke so softly in the boisterous courtroom that the court stenographer had to move his stand so that he was sitting practically in her lap. She claimed that her husband spent money lavishly on himself and his friends but often failed to cover her expenses, including her hotel bills. While she did not specifically allege marital infidelity, she testified that her husband "exhibited marked liking for actresses and others and kept pictures of them in his rooms." As evidence, she provided several "very friendly letters from women" that were read into the court record. Her charges of financial negligence and dalliances with other women rang true. Over in London, Moore had wooed Diana Manners with ermine and emeralds; back in the States, he was a deadbeat dad.

Moore did not contest the divorce. Citing his wealth and uncontroverted bad behavior, the judge awarded Elizabeth an extremely generous alimony decree that included a provision that required Moore to pay a large lump sum if he defaulted on his monthly payments. Moore was also ordered to pay off the mortgage on the house in Detroit where Elizabeth lived and give it to her free and clear. Moore could not have been pleased by the terms of the settlement, given that he was facing the loss of a substantial part of his fortune at the hands of the Investment Registry. But perhaps he didn't really care. His financial misdeeds had never stopped him from moving on to realms of greater glory. Moore made one more trip to London—perhaps to escape the publicity surrounding the salacious divorce trial—where he celebrated the Armistice along with millions of euphoric Britons.

Although Moore was free to remarry, his beloved Diana Manners was out of reach. She was engaged to Alfred Duff Cooper, a handsome young clerk in the Foreign Office. Duff, as he was known, was a notorious womanizer and a drunk who habitually gambled away most of salary. But Diana was either ignorant of Duff's shortcomings or determined not to care about them. Although the duke and duchess strongly opposed the marriage, Diana insisted that Duff was the love of her life, and they eventually acceded to Diana's wishes.

When Moore learned of the engagement, he was concerned that Duff would not be able to provide Diana the luxury to which she was accustomed. To ease the couple's financial straits, he offered to give them 6,000 pounds a year—around $533,000 in today's currency—from the time of their marriage forward. The couple initially decided it would be bad form to accept Moore's offer. But the impecunious Duff had second thoughts, writing to Diana, "The more I think about it, the more I like it." Diana sent Moore a tepid rejection of his offer, perhaps hoping to be overruled. In any event, the 6,000 pounds never materialized. Instead, Moore deposited 500 pounds in her bank account and took a box in Covent Garden in her name. Duff was disappointed. He told Diana, "I hate the opera."

Moore was to have one more European adventure before settling in America for good. In May 1918, Sir John French had been appointed Lord Lieutenant of Ireland. In that capacity, he was charged with resolving the problem of Ireland's demand for independence, a virtually impossible task. The political situation in Ireland had become steadily more explosive since the Easter Rising of 1916, when members of several Irish Republican groups took over the General Post Office in Dublin and declared a sovereign Irish republic independent of Great Britain. The British immediately put down the agitators, killing 450 people and injuring thousands more. Although the Rising was a failure, it generated widespread support for independence among Irish citizens who had been uncommitted until then. Two years later, the British Parliament voted to approve the conscription of Irish men to serve in the British army. Sinn Féin, the small but growing political party of Irish Republicans, launched a vigorous anti-conscription campaign in April 1918, joined by the Irish Party, the Labour Party, and the Catholic Church.

Sir John opposed the Irish Republicans and Sinn Féin, which he saw as a violent, extremist group that had little backing from the Irish people. Although he supported Home Rule, he believed it was necessary to quash Sinn Féin before it could be adopted. As Lord Lieutenant, he took steps to eradicate the group, arresting Sinn Féin leaders and banning all meetings of Sinn Féin's associated clubs, which he labeled "dangerous organizations." Sir John knew that Moore was an Irishman at heart and committed to securing the country's peaceful future. Aware of Moore's deftness in manipulating the press and public opinion, he enlisted his friend's assistance with the Irish Problem.

In December 1918, Sinn Féin won a landslide election, taking 75 of the 103 Irish seats in the British Parliament and replacing the Irish Party as the largest political party in Ireland. Fueled by their own success, Sinn Féin members of Parliament soon declared their own parliamentary body, the Dáil Éireann. The historic first Dáil meeting took place on January 21, 1919, at Mansion House, the residence of the Lord Mayor of Dublin. Ironically, the meeting was held in the Round Room, an enormous rotunda behind Mansion House that had been built in 1821 to accommodate the British queen on her visits.

Moore's first assignment in Ireland was to observe the Dáil Éireann's proceedings at Mansion House. At this meeting, the Dáil declared its status as the Parliament of the Irish Republic and established its own provisional government. Moore was witnessing perhaps the most important moment in Irish history: Ireland's Declaration of Independence. Although three more years would pass before the Anglo-Irish Treaty was signed and most of Ireland seceded, this meeting marked the major turning point in Ireland's fight for liberation.

Afterwards, Moore met with French to report what he had seen and heard. Hoping for stories of chaos and unruliness that would justify his insistence on eradicating Sinn Féin, French was disappointed when Moore told him that the meeting had been "perfectly orderly." And Moore went further, announcing his own support of Sinn Féin and the Irish independence movement. He told French that the group represented the "general feeling of the country" and urged French not to underestimate its resilience and deep-seated popularity. Although French knew Moore to be a shrewd judge of public opinion, he refused to accept his view of Sinn Féin. Moore's assessment proved accurate. But his advice displeased French, and his assignment in Ireland was terminated. He returned to New York in March 1919, ready to reinvent himself as a swashbuckling polo player in the festive frenzy of postwar America.

Despite the many peculiar parallels between Moore and Gatsby, their stories did not end the same way. Fitzgerald famously said that there were no second acts in American lives, a quote that has been interpreted to mean many things. Unlike Gatsby, shot dead in his swimming pool in the prime of life, Moore would live for five more decades. Like Nick Carraway and Fitzgerald himself, Moore ultimately returned to the West. His second act was set in California, another golden land of opportunity.

— CHAPTER 18 —

The Governor's Daughter

THE LEADING LADY in the opening of Moore's second act was my grandmother, Esther, his second wife. As I discovered, the story of their courtship wasn't well-known, certainly not to my mother or her brother, David. It was only recently, when I got in touch with Moore's *other* granddaughter—the daughter of Moore's first wife—that I heard the true account of how my grandparents met. It was curious, to say the least.

In 1963, my mother received a letter from a woman in Los Angeles who claimed to be her niece. The woman, Blair Sperber, known as Winky, was the daughter of Virginia Moore, Moore's daughter by his first wife. Winky was nearly the same age as my mother. She had contacted my mother in the wake of Virginia's death in the hope that my mother might be able to persuade Moore to repay the considerable sums of money that he'd inveigled from her and Virginia over the years. My mother had also suffered her father's wheedling and was hardly surprised to hear Winky's tale of woe. But she knew that getting money from her father was like getting blood from a turnip, and she told Winky so.

I got in touch with Winky in the fall of 2011. When I told her that I was writing a book about George Moore, she was astonished. In her estimation, he was a devil through and through.

The Governor's Daughter

Winky clearly bore a lot of animosity toward him that went back a long way. Most of her talk concerned my grandfather's manipulative schemes to extract money from her and her mother. Along with her many stories about Moore's unpaid debts, she revealed one intriguing fact about him that I had known nothing about. Her story involved how my grandfather happened to meet my grandmother.

My grandfather had never spent much time with his daughter Virginia. The one interest he appears to have shared with her was his passion for Irish wolfhounds. She sometimes traveled to New York with the dogs for the Westminster Kennel Club dog show. Virginia attended the Foxcroft School, a fashionable girls school in Middleburg, Virginia. Following her graduation in 1919, she settled in New York City, where she became friends with an attractive young divorcée from Boston named Esther Foss Hickman. Esther was several years older than Virginia and took the younger woman under her wing, introducing her to life in the big city. One evening they were having dinner with some of Virginia's Foxcroft friends at a midtown restaurant that Moore frequented. He happened to show up there and spent a few minutes chatting with Virginia and her friends before joining his table. Moore was instantly smitten with Esther. Like Diana Manners, she ticked all the boxes: she was beautiful, rich, and socially prominent. Shortly after this encounter, Virginia sailed from New York on her grand tour of Europe. When she returned eight months later, she learned that her father and Esther were engaged to be married.

Esther Foss Hickman, 1914

In marrying George Moore, Esther was marrying a man much like her own father and grandfather, two men straight out of the American Dream playbook. Her grandfather, Benjamin Franklin Sturtevant, was born in 1833 in a small town in central Maine where his parents eked out a living as subsistence farmers. No doubt discouraged by the prospect of spending his life digging potatoes, young Sturtevant left home in his teens to learn a trade. He found work as a shoemaker's apprentice in central Massachusetts. Soon he devised a machine for making wooden shoe pegs, and a few years later he invented a rotating exhaust fan to clear the air in his shoe-peg factory of harmful sawdust that was making the workers sick. His fan became the prototype for the modern ventilation system, and his business took off overnight. He moved the operation to Boston and built a factory in nearby Jamaica Plain. He eventually opened branches of the B. F. Sturtevant Company in New York, Chicago, Philadelphia, and London.

Esther's father, Eugene Noble Foss, was born in 1858 and raised in northern Vermont. After dropping out of college, he headed west as a traveling salesman, hawking industrial machines made by the B. F. Sturtevant Company. His impressive sales records caught Sturtevant's eye. In 1882, he summoned the young salesman to his office in Boston and offered him a position managing the company. Foss accepted the job immediately. Before long he began courting Sturtevant's 22-year-old daughter, Lilla. The couple married two years later and settled in a handsome Queen Anne–style mansion in Jamaica Plain, a wedding present from Sturtevant. Their first son, Benjamin, was born in 1886, followed three years later by another boy, Noble. Helen and Esther, the "Foss twins," were born in 1894. Because the Sturtevants had no sons, Foss's marriage to Lilla established him as heir to the family throne. When Sturtevant died unexpectedly of a stroke in 1890, Foss took over ownership of the company and was elected its president. He was thirty-two years old and, like his father-in-law, intensely ambitious.

In the early 1900s, Foss went into politics, determined to end the steep American tariffs on Canadian coal and steel that were making it costly for him to do business. After several unsuccessful campaigns for Congress, Foss ran for governor of Massachusetts as a Democrat. While few Massachusetts voters understood the intricacies of tariff reform, they all resented having to pay higher prices for Canadian coal to heat their homes during the long New England winters. Foss tapped into that sentiment and defeated his Republican opponent handily. The *New York Times* described his victory as a "landslide or earthquake, whichever it was."

Eugene Foss was a scrapper who enjoyed rough politics. Lilla sometimes took Esther and Helen to Europe when he was running for office so they would be spared the daily newspaper headlines announcing his latest dust-ups with opposing politicians. As the *Boston Post* put it, "Mrs. Foss, while very much interested in her husband's political aspirations, is averse to the attendant notoriety." As soon as Foss was elected governor, the twins' lives became fodder for the society pages. The newspapers regularly featured photographs of Esther and Helen winning prizes at horse shows, marching in parades, attending debutante balls, and appearing with their parents at official state occasions. No detail was too small to attract the press's attention. When the family attended a benefit on behalf of the Massachusetts Suffrage Society, the *Boston Globe* reported that the twins were "dressed alike in pale yellow satin, veiled with American Beauty chiffon, bordered with a fringe of gold crystals."

Foss was reelected in 1911 and 1912 (gubernatorial elections were held yearly back then) but lost his fourth bid for the governorship in 1913 and went back to private life. Around that time, Esther began seeing a young man named William Albert Hickman. Albert, as he was known, was a wealthy boat designer from Nova Scotia. He was already renowned for his invention of the "sea sled," a motorized boat with a double hull that was the precursor to the modern high-speed catamaran. Albert and Esther became engaged. They were the perfect society-page couple. One Boston newspaper reported that Esther had taken "a keen interest in her fiancé's work and some of the ideas embodied in his new boat are her own." They were married at Green Gables, the Foss's summer "cottage" in Cohasset, a wealthy resort town on the South Shore of Massachusetts.

Hickman was welcomed into the Foss family, perhaps with too much enthusiasm. Esther might have been "keen" about her husband's work, but her enthusiasm was not sufficient to hold his amorous attention. Hickman soon fell in love with Esther's sister-in-law, Dorothy Chapman Foss, the wife of Esther's oldest brother, Benjamin. The scandalous love affair between Albert and Dorothy led to double divorces for the jilted Foss siblings. Licking her wounds, Esther moved to New York City to escape the censorious wagging tongues of Boston socialites. When Virginia Moore's father showed up at the restaurant in Manhattan that fateful evening, she was ready for romance and a new husband.

"FOSS TWIN TO BE BRIDE AGAIN" read the headline in the *Boston Post* on August 30, 1921, announcing

Esther's marriage to George Moore, a "coal operator and capitalist," a "man of wealth," and an "ardent sportsman." My grandparents were married at Green Gables in the same spot where Esther had tied the knot with Albert Hickman. Only immediate members of the Foss family were present. Moore's sole representative was his polo-playing friend Willie Tevis, who had come from San Francisco to serve as best man. After the wedding breakfast, the newlyweds boarded a train for Vancouver, from where they sailed on a three-month honeymoon tour of Japan, China, and Russia.

— CHAPTER 19 —

The Golden State

M Y GRANDPARENTS RETURNED from their tour of the Far East on January 2, 1922, arriving in San Francisco aboard a ship called the *Golden State*. They planned to spend the winter and spring in California so that Moore could take part in the polo season that was just getting underway on the West Coast. Moore had staked a claim in California the previous summer by purchasing a house in Burlingame, an elite residential enclave just south of San Francisco. Not far from the house was the San Mateo Polo Club, which had stables for the club's polo ponies and a clubhouse for its members. To ensure his welcome at the club, Moore purchased the entire facility. In July 1921, before heading east for his wedding, he gave a luncheon there to introduce himself to his fellow polo enthusiasts.

A globe-trotting millionaire like Moore must have cut quite a figure in San Mateo polo circles. But the pattern of deception and delinquency that had marked his previous business practices followed him to California. His fellow club members were not amused when, on the morning of May 5, 1922, the sheriff of San Mateo County showed up at the club to attach the entire property, including polo ponies, saddles, bridles, helmets, mallets, and even the clubhouse itself. The attachment was to satisfy a $10,000 judgment against Moore, rendered in New York State court in favor of Equitable Trust Co.

The club members were outraged that the sheriff would make such an embarrassing public scene on their premises. But they were also disturbed that Moore, a newcomer with a somewhat shadowy past, had brought this scandal down on them. To add insult to injury, Moore was nowhere to be found when the sheriff arrived at the club to serve the legal papers. A few panicky telephone calls confirmed that he had gone to New York to meet his old friend Sir John French, who had come to America to see him. In Moore's absence, Esther and the club's members were left to do damage control, which involved fending off curious reporters from several newspapers, including the *New York Evening Post* and the *Oakland Tribune*. Esther and the others were said to have "expressed surprise at the attachment and belief that it would soon be lifted, as Moore's finances were in excellent condition." According to news accounts, the matter was resolved after "a hectic two days."

Moore's financial chicanery back on the East Coast was to make further waves in California. Later that summer, he was sued again, this time for failure to pay rent on Crossways, a sixty-acre estate on Long Island. An article in the *San Francisco Chronicle* titled "Polo Star Faces Another Lawsuit" got right to the point:

> Life for George Gordon Moore, multi-millionaire, son-in-law of the former Governor Foss of Massachusetts, friend of Field Marshal John French of England, and owner of the San Mateo Polo Club, is just one troublesome lawsuit after another. No sooner has Moore completed the task of placating his fellow members of the San Mateo Club after a crude deputy sheriff person attached the club, its ponies, its equipment and its

clubhouse to satisfy a judgment of $10,000 against Moore, than he is brought face to face with another suit. Now what is agitating San Mateo poloites is whether or not George Gordon Moore will come to the rescue, or whether another deputy sheriff is about to camp on the premises.

The suit was apparently settled without the need for any further visits from the sheriff. But the sheriff wasn't finished dealing with Moore. A few weeks later, Moore caused yet another stir in Burlingame when two of his Irish wolfhounds escaped from their kennel and killed a prized Toggenburg Milch goat belonging to his neighbor. This caused a feud in the neighborhood as the "goat faction" took sides against the "dog faction." It's not clear which faction won out, but it wasn't long before that would become a moot point.

Given the chaos that Moore had caused in Burlingame in just a few short months, he might have been feeling some frost from the local community. Whether moved by social pressure or the desire for more land, that summer he asked Willie Tevis to help him find a more spacious and secluded property down the California coast. Tevis's family was well-connected politically and had received many thousands of acres of land-grant property in the 1830s, including the land that eventually became William Randolph Hearst's San Simeon Ranch. Tevis's father held a controlling interest in Wells Fargo Bank, and through the bank the family had the inside scoop on available real estate all over the state.

Tevis made some inquiries and reported back to Moore. "There's a beautiful ranch for sale over in Monterey," he told him, "where the climate is as perfect as you could ask for." The property was in Carmel Valley, a few miles inland from Carmel, then a newly settled town on the Monterey Peninsula. Carmel's mild climate and extraordinary scenery had already attracted an assortment of artists and writers and other creative spirits, some of whom had fled San Francisco in 1906 after the catastrophic earthquake destroyed the city.

Just as Tevis had promised, Rancho San Carlos was spectacular. It consisted of 23,000 acres of rolling grasslands ascending into the Santa Lucia Mountains, which ran like a spine through its center. Majestic stands of redwoods sheltered trout-filled creeks that fed into the Carmel River, which flowed near the northern edge of the property. The ranch was just far enough inland to escape the fog that often shrouded the shoreline. On a clear day, Carmel Bay and Pebble Beach were visible off in the distance. It was love at first sight for Moore. He acquired title to Rancho San Carlos on July 2, 1923. The price was never recorded, but was said to be around $150,000, or less than ten dollars an acre.

Looking west over Chamisal Ridge toward the ocean

Buying Rancho San Carlos was the perfect next step for an ambitious outsider like Moore. He loved California's frontier ethos; it was the brave new world. For him, land was more powerful than a narcotic. Unlike wealth on balance sheets, land was tangible. He could see it and smell it and touch it. The more land he had, the more omnipotent he felt and the more land-hungry he became. He must have understood how satisfying it had been for his Irish-born parents—who had spent years traveling from one failed promised land to the next—to buy a few acres of land in Ontario's oil country and settle down. A decade earlier, Moore had purchased a 40,000-acre ranch in Alberta, Canada, where he installed his brother Thomas to manage a cattle operation. In the late 1920s, he acquired a ranch in Baja, Mexico, totaling 1.5 million acres. Moore named it the Circle Bar Ranch, for the brand borne by the cattle he ran there. The manager of Rancho San Carlos, who went occasionally to check on the Mexican property, described it as "incredibly wild." He added, "It goes on forever, practically from the Pacific Ocean to the Gulf of Mexico."

According to my uncle David, there was no American market for the cattle, nor was there a railroad to bring them into the country. "There was absolutely no financial benefit to owning a ranch in Mexico," he said. "He just had to have the land." In the early 1930s, Mexican Agraristas began to reclaim American-owned ranches, including the Circle Bar, for themselves and their families. Moore didn't fight the takeover. David speculated that his father had never paid for the land in the first place.

My mother inherited her father's passion for open land. Some of my earliest and happiest memories are of my mother taking me and my siblings to hike in the Blue Ridge Mountains. She taught us to fish and to identify birds. Later on, after she and my father bought their 30-acre farm in Virginia, she lamented that they hadn't settled farther out in the country, away from the relatively manicured confines of well-to-do Middleburg. She loved their farm, but she would have preferred a more remote place where they could have had hundreds of acres and raised cattle as well as horses. As a young child, I remember my parents playing a record of Ella Fitzgerald singing "Don't Fence Me In," a song that left a vivid picture in my mind's eye of the singer in a cowgirl outfit gazing out over the confines of a split-rail fence. When I hear the song now, I think about my mother and how she always yearned for a more expansive vista.

— CHAPTER 20 —

Stanway on the Pacific

THE FIRST GUESTS at Rancho San Carlos happened to be Diana Duff Cooper and her best friend, Iris Tree. They arrived in January 1927, just as the final strokes of paint were drying in Moore's newly built hacienda, which he called Casa Grande. This was an opportunity for swagger that Moore could not have imagined in his wildest dreams. He had done his best to impress Diana at the Ritz Hotel in London. Now he was ready to entertain her in his singularly American paradise on the Pacific.

Since his departure from London in 1918, Moore had continued to keep track of Diana's whereabouts. In January 1924, Diana and her husband, Duff, were in New York, where she was to appear in a revival of *The Miracle* on Broadway. After opening night, Moore showed up at the hotel where Diana and Duff were staying and invited them to dinner. Three years later, when *The Miracle* opened in San Francisco, Moore proved the soul of hospitality to Diana and Iris, who had come from England to join the cast of the play. "George Moore had come back like a good genie," Diana wrote in her memoir. "Boss of all he surveyed, he got to work on launching us socially. His magic lamp lit us and our way to adventures and parties of fabulous beauty." One such party, a dinner hosted by Moore at the Burlingame Country Club, recalled the spectacularly contrived entertainments he had hosted years earlier in London. Diana described the club's dining room as resembling "a fairy orchard in Persia at dawn. The walls, seemingly of transparent ice flushed pink, held silver espalier trees bearing golden apples." On the table for 120 guests were "tall staves on which white peacocks perched, with garlands of flowers linking them." At the corners were white china elephants "as big as genuine newborns, with white peacock-tails spreading in pride from their howdahs."

Time magazine, February 15, 1926

Moore invited Diana and Iris to Rancho San Carlos after the final performance of *The Miracle*. To make sure that Diana would be appropriately decked out for the visit, Moore presented her with a pair of luxurious riding chaps, "of piebald cowskin heavy with doubloons and silver pieces-of-eight." After arriving at Del Monte Lodge in Pebble Beach, Diana and Iris joined Moore for a horseback ride along the beach and into the breaking waves of the Pacific. The next day, they arrived at the gates of Moore's ranch, where he met them on horseback, leading two sure-footed polo ponies that were to carry the women on the nine-mile trek up to Casa Grande. "I had a tireless polo-pony that frightened me not at all," Diana wrote in a letter to Duff. "Youngster was its name." Diana was enchanted. The last five miles, she wrote, "planted with redwood trees so utterly unlike anything seen before, gave me a new lease through wonder." Rancho San Carlos is "the loveliest thing in nature," she continued. "No other dwelling in its fifty square miles. Not unlike England, quite as green, no rocks, all grass. Sometimes it's Tuscany, with ilexes springing from the swards. They look like olives grown in proportion to this large country. Hills (not mountains) and a feeling of cultivated friendliness like an orchard, though it's really as wild as on Creation Day."

Approach to the hacienda

Built in the Spanish Eclectic style, a whimsical mixture of Pueblo and Spanish Colonial Revival architecture that had come into vogue in the 1920s, Moore's hacienda was a sprawling configuration of asymmetrical wings with exposed redwood beams and colonnades stuccoed a pale gold and topped with a roof of rounded red clay tiles. It was crowned by a wide, square belvedere with three arched windows on each side. In the entry hall, the women were greeted by a glass-eyed boar's head hanging on the wall, one of Moore's hunting trophies from Hooper Bald. Straight ahead was the capacious living room, designed for hosting large parties, furnished with leather-upholstered sofas and Mission-style tables decked with horse bronzes and Asian and Native American pottery. Across from the wide stone fireplace was a wall of French doors that opened onto a terrace with a swimming pool and gardens planted by a British landscape designer. A curving stairway led from the entry hall to eight guest rooms on the second floor, each with a spectacular long view toward Monterey Bay. There was a separate wing for the nursery.

Hacienda, aerial view

Moore made sure that the hacienda was well-stocked for his guests. His wife and children had not yet moved into the new house. As Diana wrote to Duff, "the house was finished today, packed with luxury, scrumptious food and too much champagne." The United States was seven years into Prohibition, but Moore had built a concealed staircase down to the basement that held a cellar for wine and spirits. Most of his liquor came ashore on fishing boats that sailed out to British ships waiting just beyond the three-mile border of American jurisdiction. Wine was supplied by local artichoke farmers of Italian descent who produced large quantities of drinkable red. But Moore's hidden cache was more for show than necessity. He did not worry much about being raided by the feds; they were unlikely to make the trip up the long, rugged road to the house.

Diana woke early the next morning to the "nice noise of polo-balls being tapped and curses and directions." Moore and his polo team were already hard at practice on Moore's private field. After breakfast, Moore took the women on a horseback tour of the ranch that lasted most of the day. "I wanted an early bed," Diana wrote to Duff, "being bruised and longing to feel at my wellest. No such luck." Moore insisted on a full-blown evening of merriment, including a jazz chorus culled from his Black household staff. "The champagne and Bourbon flowed until 3 a.m. in such quantities that Iris and I were driven to pouring it into the grate's ashes, the flower-vases, under the sofa, anywhere, because George will not stand for anything abstemious."

Diana came upon Moore the following day drinking "vile anti-hangover concoctions." She could see that he was feeling terrible after the previous night's debauchery, but he insisted otherwise. "The climate looks after you," he told her. She was not convinced. To her dismay, another guest turned up, "a horsy mute" from Texas with ten polo ponies in tow. "He's an uneducated dreary little fourth to Iris, me and George," she wrote to Duff, "so we talked only of anthropology and

R. L. Stevenson." Diana was referring to Robert Louis Stevenson's unplanned sojourn on the ranch in the winter of 1879. Stevenson had been living in nearby Monterey, hoping to persuade his American lover, Fanny Osbourne, to leave her philandering husband and marry him. At a point when his prospects with Fanny looked dim, he had set out on a melancholy trek in the Santa Lucia Mountains. The weather was cold and wet and after a day and a night he was stricken by a recurring lung illness and collapsed. Two days later, he was discovered nearly dead lying under a tree by a goatherd named Wright who lived in a cabin with his family in a steep canyon at the southern end of the property. Wright carried him to his cabin and nursed him back to health over the course of several weeks. Stevenson's misadventure ended happily: Fanny finally dispatched her wayward husband and she and Stevenson were married the following spring. A stone chimney is all that remains of the goatherd's fabled cabin.

It was strangely fitting that Diana Duff Cooper should be the first guest at Moore's fabulous hacienda. When he had first met Diana at Stanway House fifteen years earlier, Moore was a bold, rough-hewn American finding his footing in unfamiliar social territory. He did his best to comport himself like a proper Edwardian gentleman, but to him, the nobody from nowhere, the air must have felt a bit thin in those rarified drawing rooms. In Carmel, the tables were turned. Casa Grande was his version of Stanway House on the wild western frontier. He had not had the good fortune to inherit a magnificent manor house, but he had something much more impressive: Rancho San Carlos was a monument to his own self-made success.

Diana and Iris's visit was the first of a nearly constant flow of guests to Rancho San Carlos over the course of California's

January-to-May polo season. Near the hacienda were private cottages for Averell Harriman, Tommy Hitchcock, and other polo players who came for the season. Guests came from everywhere—Argentina, Great Britain, New York, Texas—to revel in Moore's celebrated hospitality. Life at Rancho San Carlos became a round-the-clock party, with Moore the beaming Lord of Misrule. Champagne corks popped from dusk till dawn. Polo players played hard and partied harder. According to one local, "the ranch *was* the social center of Carmel Valley for a while, particularly with the likes of Harriman and Hitchcock and the Hollywood people coming and going. Moore seemed quite the buccaneer, with a very beautiful wife."

George Moore, c. 1928

As in New York, Moore and his parties were the subject of racy gossip. Some people claimed that his Argentinian polo friends lured girls up to Casa Grande with promises of bootleg liquor and introductions to Hollywood moguls and then held them captive. Moore was suspected of installing peepholes behind the bookshelves so that he could spy on people making love in the living room. It seems a bit farfetched to imagine that Moore's guests couldn't find more private places than the living room for such intimacies, but the rumor reflected Moore's scandalous reputation, which endured through the decades. (The long-held speculation that Moore was the bastard son of British royalty became solidly rooted in local lore. A newspaper clipping from the Monterey County Library archives announcing my mother's marriage in 1949 bore the scribbled note "Nephew of Ed. VIII" next to Moore's name.)

After the polo season, things quieted down until late August, when Moore held his annual barbecue in the 1,200-acre redwood grove. The entertainment included boxing matches, dancing girls, and two orchestras providing nonstop music. These fêtes took weeks to prepare, since the tables and chairs, the dance floor, and the boxing ring had to be brought in pieces by wagon to the distant site. The meat, all raised on the ranch, was cooked over a sunken barbecue pit as long as a shuffleboard court. Liquor flowed freely. More than 400 guests came, some from Hollywood, including Helen Hayes, Mary Pickford, and Douglas Fairbanks Jr. Also on the guest list was Arnold Genthe, the German-born photographer who became famous for chronicling the 1906 San Francisco earthquake in pictures. Genthe's series of photographs of the 1927 barbecue captured its exotic, enchanted gaiety. In one, a Spanish dancer clad in a slinky black dress and high heels stamps her feet on a raised stage surrounded by party guests. Another shows a group of Black servants in white chef's toques and aprons shrouded in smoke as they hover over the barbecue pit with long sharp sticks tending to huge cauldrons of food and thick slabs of meat. The photographs connote a vaguely colonial atmosphere; the party might have taken place on a plantation in Africa.

Chefs working over the fire pit, 1927

Boxing match at barbecue, 1927

— CHAPTER 21 —
A 23,000-Acre Playground

MOORE'S FINEST MOMENT in polo is memorialized in a photograph of him and his teammates Tommy Hitchcock, Averell Harriman, and Willie Tevis, after winning the 1929 Pacific Coast Polo Championship, the most prestigious tournament in the West. The picture shows the victorious San Carlos Cardinals standing on the battered polo field with a stylish young woman who is presenting the ornate trophy that is nearly as tall as they are. The woman is Lady Alexandra Metcalfe, daughter of Lord Curzon, Viceroy of India, where modern polo was born. She is the epitome of 1920s chic; her low-cut print silk dress barely grazes her knees, a cloche hat frames her angular face, and a fur-trimmed coat hugs her slender silhouette. The players still appear to be breathing hard as they stand before the camera. They hold their individual trophies, long-stemmed silver goblets, casually at their sides, as if they were polo mallets. Their hair is uncombed and sweat-slicked. Hitchcock and Moore wear double-breasted polo coats, the latest fashion, over their jerseys and britches. The photograph appeared in newspapers all over the country.

Presentation of the Pacific Coast Polo Championship trophy, 1929

Moore had every reason to be proud that day. Reporting on the final match, the *New York Times* noted that "George Gordon Moore, the lowest ranked member of the team, came through in the seventh chukker rush, which placed the ball in good position for Hitchcock to score the final goal, securing the game and title." Despite his limitations on the polo field, Moore never had trouble attracting top players for his team. He was a significant presence in the polo world, on the field and off. When the United States sent a polo team led by Tommy Hitchcock to the 1924 Olympic Games in Paris, Moore was named as an alternate. This was probably a courtesy designation, acknowledging that he had supplied several ponies for the American team. The Americans played triumphantly but gave up the gold medal to Argentina after Hitchcock was injured during the final match. After the games Moore purchased several of the victorious Argentinians' best ponies and shipped them home to Carmel.

The glory days of the San Carlos Cardinals had begun two years earlier, in January 1927, when Moore, Hitchcock, Harriman, and a new teammate, a young Irishman named Aidan Roark, headed down to Los Angeles to play in a tournament at the Midwick Country Club. At age 22, Roark was already well-known, having played for Ireland in international competition. Roark and his brother Pat had first come to America to play on Long Island in the mid-1920s. Impressed by their finesse on the field, Moore invited them to bring their polo talents out to California.

Although the Cardinals had played in many tournaments, the Midwick tournament was particularly momentous. With his polo operation at Rancho San Carlos up and running, Moore finally had his own home team. The Cardinals won the tournament. Diana Duff Cooper had come to the closing match, making the victory especially sweet for Moore. Hitchcock, by far the best player on the team, was thrilled with his teammates' performance. In a letter to his father, he reported that Moore and Roark had "played better than they knew how" and that Harriman "was riding harder and doing more work."

Moore's installations at Hooper Bald and in St. Clair, Michigan, had been mere rehearsals for Rancho San Carlos. He envisioned the ranch as a sporting paradise where he and his guests could ride horses, play polo, and hunt during the day and then party long into the night. He spared no expense. The hacienda included a billiard room on the first floor and a gym in the basement where Moore trained as a boxer, a sport he pursued avidly. He built a tennis court and swimming pool as well as kennels for his Irish wolfhounds and other hunting dogs. He dammed a creek to create an eighteen-acre lake and a fish hatchery. In addition to the polo operation, he began breeding Thoroughbred horses for racing. He built a separate fifty-stall barn and a half-mile racetrack where his horses could train. Although most states, including California, banned Thoroughbred racing at the time, it was legal in Mexico. Along with other wealthy Californians, including Charles and Marcella Howard, owners of the legendary racehorse Seabiscuit, he sent his horses across the border to run at Tijuana's fashionable Agua Caliente racetrack.

The polo compound

Rancho San Carlos also provided ideal terrain for boar hunting without the problems of maintenance and accessibility that had plagued Hooper Bald. Moore asked Cotton McGuire, his former manager at Hooper Bald, to round up twelve boars, three males and nine females—the same number he had imported from Russia in 1910—and bring them by train across the country to the ranch. McGuire may well have regretted his agreement to undertake such a dangerous and difficult task, but he did it. Three hounds were killed and one man badly injured in trapping the boars on Hooper Bald. McGuire somehow managed to wrangle the beasts onto the train; five days later, they all arrived with much fanfare in Carmel. McGuire stayed at the ranch for several weeks, during which time Moore tried to persuade him to move out to California with his family to manage the ranch. But McGuire declined. He told Moore that his wife refused to leave North Carolina, but back in Robbinsville he explained things differently. "I liked the place," he said, "but not the people."

Moore eagerly introduced boar hunting to his California friends and visitors. He claimed that the largest boar he ever killed on the ranch was nine feet from nose to tail. "The skin on his neck was three inches thick," he wrote in his 1963 letter to Stuyvie Fish. "Eleven bullets were found which over the years had been embedded in the fat." As if boar hunting with rifles and hounds was not thrilling enough, some of Moore's more foolhardy friends took up his challenge to go "pig-sticking." The pursuit—could it even be called a sport?—is as crude as its name suggests: men on horseback roust boars from their lairs and chase after them, trying to gore them with long, sharp spears.

Like other activities Moore pursued, pig-sticking was popular with British officers in India in the late 19th and early 20th centuries. According to Lt.-Colonel Arthur Brooke, who wrote a treatise on the subject in 1920, it "was encouraged by military authorities as good cavalry training because of the degree of horsemanship required, and because of the cunning and ferocity of the boar." Brooke noted that well-trained polo ponies made excellent pig-stickers, because they were "handy as a cat and hard as iron." For those wanting to take up the sport, he advised buying a quality helmet. Good weapons, he added, were equally important. "Your spear should be carefully selected, with a good head and a good strong male bamboo shaft," he wrote. "Above all have your spears as sharp as razors and their points like needles." I wonder whether the pig-stickers at Rancho San Carlos were equipped to Brooke's specifications. As far as I know, no humans died on the hunt. Perhaps no boars did either.

For slightly saner guests, Moore offered a game of archery on horseback. This involved riders galloping around the polo field with a bow and arrow slung across their backs, taking aim at a target as they rode past, faster and faster with each lap. Like polo, the sport required excellent horsemanship and daring. One of the most avid mounted archers was Lord Wodehouse, third Earl of Kimberley, a top international polo player, who stayed with Moore during the 1926 polo season. (A distant cousin of the writer P. G. Wodehouse, Lord Wodehouse was apparently the model for Bertie Wooster, the befuddled aristocrat in the classic Jeeves stories.) Lord Wodehouse took great pleasure in the game and promised to open several clubs in England when he returned home later in the year. Moore also staged paper chases, the game known in England as "hare and hounds," on horseback. One rider, designated as the hare, would take off over a course of difficult terrain as fast as he could, dropping shreds of paper—the "scent"—for the other riders, the hounds, to track. Several years earlier, before Moore's dinner honoring Diana Duff Cooper at the Burlingame Club, he had invited the guests to take part in such a paper chase. Diana described it in a letter to Duff as "nerve-destroying" and reported that Iris had been "tossed high in the air" as she navigated the trail. Moore reveled in this sort of high-risk high jinks. He had no concern for the safety of those he involved in his dangerous pastimes. The players were there for his amusement. In his view—to borrow a legal phrase—they "assumed the risk."

— CHAPTER 22 —

Empty Promises

To Moore, business was a sport like any other. He approached it with the same recklessness he exhibited on the playing field. With the All-American warrior-athlete Tommy Hitchcock as his right-hand man, he had no trouble attracting wealthy investors for his promotions. His portfolio of public utilities, including United Electric Coal Co. and Georgia Railway and Power Co., provided more than ample income to support his lavish lifestyle. But Moore loved to gamble and he put much of his investors' cash into riskier boom-or-bust operations. Hitchcock's social cachet was indispensable to Moore's schemes. Although Hitchcock was young and naïve, his sterling reputation gave investors confidence that their money was in good hands. Hitchcock's lack of experience also worked in Moore's favor; a savvier associate would have immediately recognized that Moore was playing fast and loose with other people's money.

But Hitchcock caught on eventually. Several years into their business relationship, he began to doubt the propriety of Moore's operations. According to Nelson Aldrich, Hitchcock had rather obliquely communicated his doubts about Moore to an old army friend, Bill Wellman, who had become a successful movie director in Hollywood. In 1928, when Hitchcock was in Los Angeles for a polo tournament, he had dinner with Wellman. Many years later, Wellman told

Aldrich about this meeting. In his biography of Hitchcock, Aldrich recounted what Wellman had said to him:

> There was something about [Hitchcock] that was sad, unhappy. . . . I could tell he was really serious because now and then he had a stuttering way of talking. Not really a stutter, just a momentary thing: "Butabutabut . . ." That sort of thing. And he stuttered then when he said, "Bill, this working with George Moore, what do you think of it?"
> Christ, I didn't know what to say. I thought Tom was great. I didn't know Moore personally, but from what I'd heard about him, I was sure I hadn't missed anything. So I told Tom he was terrific and we let it go. But it was bothering him, I could tell, and plenty. You know, a lot of people used to say he was never scared. Hell, he wasn't nuts. Of course he was scared sometimes. He just controlled it, that's all. It was the same way with his other feelings, like his worries about working with Moore. He hid them, but he had them.

It appears that Hitchcock had reason to be uneasy. Aldrich referred to "rumors of gold mines with no gold in them and oil wells with no oil," but concluded that "there are no facts to go on." Actually, there are some facts. One of Moore's businesses was Siosi Oil, an oil-drilling operation on several thousand acres of leased oil fields south of Terre Haute, Indiana. In 1927, the state of Indiana sued Siosi Oil for grossly understating the amount of capital it had invested in the oilfield in order to avoid paying fees owed to the state for conducting business there. In January 1929, another lawsuit charged the company with creating a fake oil well. Siosi had allegedly piped gas from one property to another to make it appear that it had drilled a well there, as required by contract with the property owner.

As a teammate, Hitchcock admired Moore's brazen conduct on the polo field. But in business, he expected Moore to stick to the rules. He knew that Moore's reckless disregard for the law could bring them both down. In 1928 Hitchcock bowed out, accepting an offer from his North Shore neighbor Robert Lehman to work in New York at Lehman Brothers investment banking firm. But whatever misgivings Hitchcock had about Moore's business practices, the two remained on good terms, and he continued as the powerhouse of the San Carlos Cardinals even after the stock market crash of 1929.

What kept Hitchcock and the other high-goal players suiting up for Moore's team year after year? They would have been welcomed by any other team on the West Coast. It certainly wasn't the quality of Moore's playing, which was far below the level of his teammates. Did people know about his crooked business dealings? At Casa Grande, where champagne flowed like water, people didn't ask too many questions. As long as Moore's money held out and the parties continued, everyone was happy to be his friend.

— CHAPTER 23 —

Childhood at Rancho San Carlos

On August 7, 1923, a few weeks after Moore purchased the ranch, Esther gave birth to my mother, Sheilah Blair, in San Mateo. My uncle, David Gordon, was born sixteen months later, on December 4, 1924. My grandfather hadn't been much of a father to Virginia; his second time around as a parent was not much better. He joined the family in California for the polo season, January through May, but polo and parties left him little time for his children. The rest of the year he was in New York, where his business operations were based, or on the road in search of new mining opportunities. "The lure of the New York business world was everything to him," said David. "It wasn't like, 'Oh, Christ, I've gotta go to work now.' He was dying to get into the act."

Esther spent a lot of time with her twin sister, Helen, who had moved to Pebble Beach in the early 1920s with her husband, Whitman Hobbs, another wealthy Bostonian. Helen and Whitman had three young children who played with Sheilah and David while their mothers amused themselves. Esther quickly made friends with Carmel locals, including the celebrated poet Robinson Jeffers and his wife, Una.

Until Casa Grande was completed in 1927, Esther and the children lived in Pebble Beach. They spent a couple of months each winter with Moore in New York. During the summer, they visited Esther's family in Cohasset. Like most wealthy women of her day, Esther was not a hands-on mother or housekeeper. She had a staff that included a German nanny named Emma Meith, who lived with the children in the nursery wing of Casa Grande. The separation between the children and their parents was personal as well as spatial. "In those days Emma did everything for us," said David. "We were presented to our parents at special times and that was it."

Left to right: Moore's valet, John Raming, the children's nurse, Emma Meith, David, and Sheilah, c. 1927

Much later, Emma became a figure in my life too. She never left the family, eventually retiring to a cottage on the Fish Ranch, where Uncle Stuyvie lived. We spent several summers in Carmel during my childhood. My mother had always been close to Stuyvie, and we often visited him at the ranch. He was a handsome, humorous man who always seemed pleased with himself. I remember him telling us children with great enthusiasm that he had once pissed in the prince of Germany's beer. I have no idea when or how this might have occurred, but I imagined a tall glass of beer sitting untended on a table in a German palace while Stuyvie unzipped his fly and looked to see if the coast was clear.

Stuyvie had recently begun to domesticate the boars that had strayed from Rancho San Carlos and to market the meat as a delicacy. When we visited, he gave us bags of stale bread to feed the baby boars. They were so adorable it was hard to believe they could ever grow up to be the fearsome, nasty-looking beasts that fixed their beady eyes on us and snorted through the strands of their separate barbed-wire pens. We climbed into the babies' enclosure and fed them by hand and stroked their wiry spotted coats until we were overcome by the stink of the pens. (Stuyvie's boar business never took off. As it turned out, he was about fifty years ahead of his time. Nonetheless, every year he sent my parents a crate of cured boar meat. I found the taste revolting, but my mother served it at dinner parties, to the amusement and horror of the guests. Most of it went to our basset hounds, who camped under the table at dinnertime.)

From the pens we made our way to Emma's cottage, taking time to chase azure-bellied lizards that darted lightning-fast along the split-rail fences that edged the path. Emma shared the cottage with a prim Scottish woman named Belle, who had been my grandmother's personal maid. The old ladies doted on us as if we were their own grandchildren, giving us candy and jelly jars full of fresh milk from the ranch's dairy. I dreaded having to drink the milk; I couldn't stop thinking of the distended pink udders of the cows in the dairy barn. But I loved hearing Emma's stories of our mother's heroics on horseback—for example, how she would ride standing on her horse's rump, or jump her horse over a picnic table set with dishes and food. She told us about sending Sheilah and David off on days-long rides with the cowboys to round up cattle that had been let loose in the mountains. She said she was forever reminding the children not to let their mother know what they'd been up to. "Ach, don't tell your mother!" she would repeat to us, laughing to herself. I don't think she worried they would tell; it was no mystery where the children's loyalties lay.

Apart from Emma's tales, I never knew much about my mother's early life. Her childhood looms in my mind like a perplexing fairy tale or a vivid, half-remembered dream. Most of my impressions come from photographs and paintings from those years. I have some of these works in the original, including a series of oil portraits of my mother as a young child. These were painted by an Italian portraitist, Count Giulio de Blaas, who visited the family every Christmas. Lulo, as he was known, painted my mother first as a somber-faced baby holding a green rubber ball, then as a chubby red-cheeked toddler holding a wild-eyed doll, and later as melancholy youngster with huge, sad blue eyes the same color as the ribbons tied in her curly brown hair.

The third portrait evokes an unhappy childhood memory I have of my siblings and me sitting for our own portraits, rendered in pastel. I was five or six years old. I have no idea who the artist was—Lulo was long dead by then—but I recall my fearfulness at being placed by myself in a room with a thickly accented middle-aged man I'd never seen before. The experience lingers uneasily in my mind in the same nightmare-memory portal as childhood visits to the dentist. Looking at my mother's sad-eyed portrait, done at about the same age I was when I sat for mine, I imagine her discomfort at being staged like a doll in an adult's puppet show. That was certainly how I felt when my portrait was made.

A series of photographic portraits of young Sheilah and David, made by Julian P. Graham, a well-known photographer of California society and sporting life, convey the same aura of "presentation" formality. One of his photographs, taken shortly after the family moved into Casa Grande, shows my mother, aged about seven, sitting back-to-back with David on the patio by the swimming pool. Because my grandmother was herself a twin, she always dressed the children in matching outfits. In this photograph, they are dressed in blouses and short pants over long white socks and black patent-leather Mary Janes. My mother poses self-consciously, with one knee bent, the other leg stretched out, gazing solemnly down at the water, as if searching for a sunken keepsake. In the foreground, rising from the pool, is a statue of a young nude woman holding a wreath of flowers high above her head. Her risqué presence suggests that the pool was not meant as a play area for small children.

Another photograph shows the children posed in front of a tall split-rail fence. They are dressed in rumpled blue jeans and matching woolen cardigans with patch pockets and leather buttons, like something an old man might wear. On their feet are scuffed, high-laced shoes. My mother has her arm stiffly around David's shoulder. She is a picture of misery. She stares into Graham's camera as if facing down an executioner. The opulent Casa Grande is visible in the background, but the photograph could easily be one of Walker Evans's grim depictions of 1930s deprivation. Graham also captured an image of the children posed in the same spot with their grandfather, Eugene Foss, who had traveled west to visit his daughters and their families. The former governor of Massachusetts looks clownish in his heavily ornamented leather chaps, cowboy boots, and cowboy-style kerchief. The children stand on either side of him dutifully holding his hands. They look bewildered, as if they have been posed with a giant cardboard cutout of a cowpoke at a Wild West show. I like to think that Foss enjoyed his visit with the family. He was said to have been a playful and fun-loving parent back in the day. But there's no trace of pleasure or warmth on those three grim faces.

Sheilah and David with their maternal grandfather,
Eugene Noble Foss, c. 1928

The pictorial record suggests that the children were considerably happier in the presence of horses and dogs. A cheerier photograph shows the children in the nursery, sitting contentedly in their highchairs at the breakfast table. At the table with them, facing the camera, is a fluffy black and white dog named Willy. Like the children, he is wearing a bib and has a plate of food in front of him. I can't imagine how Graham managed to get Willy to sit for more than a few seconds in this upright position with his paws on the table. Perhaps, under Emma's indulgent care, he was a regular guest at meals.

Childhood at Rancho San Carlos

Sheilah and David with Willy at breakfast

Children in barn doorway

I think it was mostly a blessing for my mother and David that their parents were too involved with their own lives to pay much attention to them. The children learned to ride as soon as they could walk. They hung out with the cowboys and worked cattle, broke horses, and helped with the enormous job of haymaking. One photograph shows the children at ages six and seven in matching cowboy outfits with their piebald Shetland pony, Dusty Foot. David sits proudly in the big Western saddle while my mother stands beside the pony, with one hand on his face and the other on his bridle. She looks purposeful and alert, as if she's making sure that the pony doesn't misbehave. The happiest photograph of all shows my mother and David riding their horses through a meadow of wildflowers. The horses are fat and shiny. My mother has a big smile on her face. The picture could be titled "Children in Paradise."

Children in Paradise

In some respects, the ranch *was* a paradise. The children didn't go to school. No matter what their parents were up to, Emma was there for them. There were several events in the year that they looked forward to, including the annual barbecue in the hallowed Redwood Grove. They were too young to stay for long, but they were allowed to watch guests assemble and to throw sticks into the fiery barbecue pit. Even at that young age, they knew that the parties were opportunities for grown-up misbehavior. David recalled that some guests would pass out in the brush and come straggling up to the house in the morning as he and my mother were eating their breakfast.

But the children's years at Rancho San Carlos wouldn't last much longer. Marital strife and financial catastrophe were just around the corner. As the Roaring Twenties faded into the twilight, an ominous new decade was dawning.

— CHAPTER 24 —

The Foss Twins Behave Badly

B Y 1929, THE SAN CARLOS CARDINALS had established themselves as one of the West Coast's leading teams. The polo season that year promised to be Moore's biggest and best ever. As play got underway in early January, Moore welcomed several houseguests to Casa Grande. Among them were his young Irish teammate, Aidan Roark, who lived in Los Angeles the rest of the year, and Captain Henry Forester, a British polo champion and cavalry officer who had come from his home in Salisbury, England, to play on the California winter circuit.

Forester was good-looking, wealthy, and single. One afternoon when he was coming in from practice he happened to catch the eye of Esther's sister, Helen, who was visiting for the day. She was instantly enthralled by the debonair Brit, as he was by her. Soon the two began to have secret trysts, most likely encouraged and facilitated by Esther. The affair blossomed into a full-blown romance. Within the year, Helen divorced Whitman Hobbs and married Henry Forester in a quiet wedding at Rancho San Carlos.

With two young children and an older, preoccupied husband, it's easy to imagine that Esther envied her twin's illicit romance. When Moore was away, which was most of the time, Rancho San Carlos was very quiet. I doubt the children minded, though it must have been a bit dull for my cosmopolitan grandmother. The famous Foss twins had been copycats since birth, always dressing in matching outfits, attending the same schools and parties, participating in the same activities. As adults, they continued to live their lives in tandem on the California coast. When Helen took up with an international polo player, was Esther tempted to follow suit? An adulterous affair with a polo player would be the ultimate act of imitation.

George and Esther Moore, c. 1929

Rancho San Carlos was the perfect incubator for sexual mischief. Esther found a playmate right there at Casa Grande. Aidan Roark was twenty-five years old, ten years younger than Esther, but the age gap was evidently no barrier to their attraction. It's easy to understand what Esther saw in the "Irish polo ace," as Una Jeffers referred to him. Unlike Moore, he was strikingly handsome. He had undeniable sex appeal, exuding Irish wit and charm. He was the perfect catch for an older woman looking for a romantic fling. It's less clear what attracted Roark to Esther. Money and good looks, of course. But how did her marriage to Moore figure in his thinking? Did it tip the scales in favor of the affair or against it? Moore was old enough to be his father. Roark might have privately judged him as a vain and mediocre polo player who stooped to buying talent for his team. But whatever Roark thought of the older man, Moore was essentially his boss. Stealing Moore's wife might have seemed ill-advised under the circumstances. But it was also an uncompromisingly macho move befitting a young polo star like Roark.

George Moore and Aidan Roark, March 1930

Did my grandfather know about the affair? Did he care? Roark was one of the best players in the West. His talent made up for Moore's deficiencies on the field. Regardless of what Moore knew and when he knew it, there's no evidence of any rift between the two men as far as polo was concerned. Roark continued to play for the Cardinals every year through the 1931 season. In March 1931, at a popular horse race meeting in Santa Cruz, Roark rode one of Moore's polo ponies, a mare named Nellie Bly, to second place in a half-mile race. He may well have stayed at Rancho San Carlos during that year's polo season.

The Foss Twins Behave Badly

By the summer of 1931 Esther's relationship with Roark was out in the open. She declared an official separation and moved off the ranch, taking David and Sheilah, aged seven and eight, to live in Pebble Beach. For the first time in their lives they went to school. It must have been a big adjustment, although my mother never talked about it. Leaving the ranch was difficult for them. "We were cowboys," said David. "All we wanted to do was ride all over creation. We really missed that." A photograph of them with their mother after the separation captures their grim mood. Dressed in matching polka-dotted outfits, they stare out past the camera. David appears to be doing his best to fight off tears. My mother looks like she's already cried her eyes out. Esther, dressed in black with a simple string of pearls around her neck, sits between them. Her jaw is set, her eyes are steely. She holds my mother's hand stiffly; her other arm is around David's waist. I cannot imagine what prompted her to have the portrait made at such a fraught moment in the children's lives. Perhaps she was trying to create a picture of normalcy in what was a most abnormal situation.

Esther and the children, c. 1931

Two years later, Esther took the children to live in Reno, Nevada, for two months so she could get a quick divorce. On April 4, 1933, her divorce petition was filed, fueling society pages far and wide. Reflecting Moore's erstwhile financial triumphs, news reports described him as a "coal baron," "California millionaire and polo player," "New York sportsman," and "Detroit traction magnate." The divorce was granted after a brief private hearing on grounds of non-support. Before the suit was heard, the couple made a property settlement and agreed that Esther would have exclusive custody of the children. Moore was in no position to take care of the children, but Esther was scarcely better suited for the task.

"FOSS DAUGHTER TAKES POLO STAR AS NO. 3" read the headline in the *Boston Daily Record* announcing my grandmother's marriage to Aidan Roark. The wedding took place in early January 1934, nine months after the Reno divorce. The ceremony was hosted by Sidney and Olga Fish, Stuyvie's parents, at their Palo Corona Ranch. The Fishes had been close friends of my grandparents before the divorce, and they took Esther's side when the marriage broke up. To add insult to injury, the Fish ranch was just next door, so to speak, to Rancho San Carlos. What was my grandfather feeling as he sat alone in his Casa Grande, knowing that his former wife was marrying the slick young polo player whom he had brought to California a few years earlier? Was he angry, or humiliated, or both?

After the wedding, Esther took my mother and David to live in Beverly Hills. Roark was working in Hollywood for the producer Darryl Zanuck, an avid polo player who had hired Roark mainly for his talent on the polo field. As Tommy Hitchcock's biographer observed, "The successful in Hollywood were frantic for 'class.' Movie people took to polo much as they took to aristocrats. It was a 'class' game, and though most of them played badly, they played enthusiastically." Zanuck certainly came out of this mold.

He had recently left Warner Brothers to form 20th-Century Pictures, and his new operation was going well enough that he could afford to hand out plum jobs to people who would lend cachet to his office. Zanuck assigned Roark to read movie scripts. He told one of his associates, "If Aidan understands a script, it should be crystal clear to a ten-year-old kid sitting in the front seat at a movie. Anyway, think what it means to our prestige, having a ten-goal man on our payroll."

From what little my mother said about this period of her life, I gather it was not very happy. I knew two things about her sojourn in Beverly Hills. First, she got to know the young movie star Lana Turner while sunbathing at a local country club. (Turner, two years older than my mother, had been famously discovered by Warner Brothers' director Mervyn LeRoy in 1936, at age sixteen, while having a soda at the Top Hat malt shop in Hollywood.) Second, avocado trees grew in their backyard, and the family ate avocados at every meal to economize on household expenses. Avocados—my mother called them "alligator pears"—were a delicacy in our house when I was growing up. A limitless supply of avocados seemed like nothing to complain about. But my mother told us it had taken her many years to regain her appetite for avocados.

It's unlikely that the Roarks' finances were so tight they needed to supplement the family's diet with homegrown avocados. Even though the Depression was in full swing, Roark was a well-paid Hollywood executive. I think my mother's complaint about being fed an unvarying diet of avocados reflected her disapproval of Esther's priorities. My mother insinuated that Esther wasn't the type to stint on fancy gowns or stylish hats, but feeding her children properly was another matter.

Unsurprisingly, my grandmother's marriage to Roark was a disaster. They separated on October 1, 1937, less than four years after their wedding. She and the children moved back to Carmel, and she filed for divorce on grounds of cruelty two months later. The complaint was heard in open court and widely covered by the press. A photograph of Esther looking pallid and tight-lipped appeared in the *Los Angeles Times* accompanying an article that began "Affirmative monosyllables yesterday comprised the principal testimony of Mrs. Esther F. Roark when she obtained an interlocutory decree of divorce from Aidan Roark, polo-playing scenario writer."

The picture of the marriage that emerged from the divorce papers is of two grown-ups behaving like petty, spoiled children. The scenes my grandmother described in court could have come from a Hollywood screwball comedy, except that there was no kissing and making up at the end. Among other particulars, my grandmother charged that Roark "neglected her socially and refused to co-operate with her in work to be done in their home." It's not clear what work my grandmother wanted to have done. She was accustomed to living in grand houses, and Roark was not a wealthy man. Did she insist on installing a sunken marble bathtub with gold-plated faucets, or was she merely asking for furniture or separate bedrooms for the children?

Esther also claimed that Roark was "rude to her in the presence of friends and would play the radio at odd hours of the day and night." Playing the radio at odd hours is hardly enough to bring the curtain down on a marriage. But it seems there was a hostile edge to the radio playing. Eleanor Walsh, a friend of Esther's, testified that Roark once turned on the radio just as her husband was about to tell a story. I can imagine Roark playing the radio in a fit of passive-aggressive petulance, perhaps to drown out his wife's complaining. Then again, he might have done it just to annoy her.

The most egregious cruelty allegedly inflicted by Roark occurred on Thanksgiving Day, 1936, when he and Esther were driving from Carmel to Beverly Hills, a trip that would have taken more than six hours. According to my grandmother, Roark refused to put up the top on his convertible, even though—or perhaps because—it was pouring rain and windy, and she was suffering from a bad cold. What had Esther done to provoke Roark to behave like such a lout? Roark was known to have a temper. He once was reported to have had a "fistic encounter" with Errol Flynn. But he got as cold and wet as she did, after all.

Zanuck eventually fired Roark in the early 1940s. The final straw was a memo Roark wrote for Zanuck that described a script as "a machinegun-paced comedy that seems to drag a little." Zanuck's response to this was, "Jesus, that's the first time I've ever seen anyone do a U-turn in the middle of a sentence." The official reason for Roark's dismissal was that he had become "too sophisticated."

I knew that my grandmother's marriage to Roark had been brief, but I was surprised that the relationship had been so acrimonious. I don't recall my mother ever saying anything bad about Roark. He shared my parents' interest in racehorses and served for many years as a steward at Santa Anita racetrack. My mother stayed in touch with him and his subsequent wife, the renowned tennis champion Helen Wills Moody, until their deaths many years later. Remarking on the callous disregard with which her mother had left my grandfather and Roark, my mother said, "We didn't even get a chance to say goodbye to them."

— CHAPTER 25 —

Decline and Fall

Moore's marital troubles were nothing compared to the financial disaster he faced in the wake of the stock market collapse of October 1929. Although the crash did not bring about his immediate ruin, my grandfather knew that his financial empire was heading over a cliff. He continued to keep up appearances for a couple of years, staying one jump ahead of his creditors. Capital to fuel his mineral explorations dried up. He was up to his ears in debt. He continued to hemorrhage money. He was said to have lost $8 million in a single month.

Moore did his best to keep up appearances. Peggy Hitchcock recalled that he continued having parties in New York. "He wanted so badly to hold on to the gay, old times," she told Aldrich. "It was rather pathetic. He tried so hard to hold it all together, and finally, later, he lost everything." A sure sign that Moore's high times were over came at one his legendary parties in New York City, probably his last. Peggy and Tommy Hitchcock were among the guests enjoying a fancy dinner when all the lights went out. Apparently, Moore was months behind on his electric bills and the company had finally cut him off. The guests hurriedly got up from the table and fumbled in the dark for their hats and coats. As gracefully as they could, they stepped out onto 52nd Street like mink-clad rats off a sinking ocean liner.

A 1932 gossip column in the *New York World-Telegram* titled "Court Jester's Cap Worn Here No More," proclaimed the end of Moore's reign over New York high society:

> The life of a court jester isn't an easy one. He is liable to become as out of date as yesterday's newspaper. In predepression times George Moore supplied ideas for Park Avenue in its off moments. He snapped the whip to the tune of "On with the Dance!" Mr. Moore may be said to have been the last to wear the cap and bells. Four years ago he was on the crest of the Social Register wave. Today he is forgotten. At the peak of the stock market his house in 52nd St. was known to all of fashionable New York, his estate at Sands Point a gathering spot for polo-playing Long Island, and his parties the focal point for the young and sophisticated smart set.
>
> A year or so ago, he went West. Mrs. Charles Amory bought his Long Island place. No one seems to know what became of the 52nd St. house.
>
> Mr. Moore might have been called more than a court jester. For a time he played the part of dictator.

By the time this biting notice appeared, Moore's money had run out. For a man who had thrived for so many years on luxury, power, and lively companionship, financial ruin hit hard. Operations at Rancho San Carlos were falling apart. In June 1933, the California labor commissioner attached the ranch for back wages owed to 21 employees. In 1934, New York Telephone and Telegraph Company sued him for unpaid charges totaling more than $6,000. In 1935, he declared bankruptcy. There were most certainly other lawsuits charging Moore with deceit, but the defrauded plaintiffs knew that there would be little or no money to recoup. In bankruptcy, Moore was, in legal terms, judgment proof.

Throughout the 1930s Moore managed to hang onto the ranch and maintain some semblance of a social life there, recreating as best he could the high times he'd enjoyed during the preceding decade. The most clear-eyed account of life on the ranch in the 1930s came from a woman named Carol Baudouin who worked as my grandfather's secretary and bookkeeper for a year or so. Baudouin had escaped the Oklahoma Dust Bowl to live with her sister in Monterey. Her brother-in-law, who worked for the phone company, heard that Moore was looking for someone to do office work for him and mentioned this to her. She borrowed his Chevrolet and headed to the ranch for an interview. She was greeted by a one-legged gatekeeper who lived in a shack at the entrance to the ranch. "I was scared," she said.

Moore offered Baudouin the job and a bedroom on the first floor of Casa Grande. She returned a few days later with her belongings. When she opened the closet to put away her clothes, a jumble of polo mallets spilled out. Baudouin recalled that Moore was always short of money. Her pay often came in the form of turkeys, chickens, eggs, and wood that she took to her sister on weekends. Sometimes, she said, Moore would call her and the cowboys into his bedroom first thing in the morning and give them the day's instructions while lying in bed in his pajamas. One day, my grandfather told her to go through his library and cull all the first editions; she figured he meant to sell them.

Moore's valet and chauffeur, John Raming, was a wiry Bahamian known to the family as Old Black John. My grandfather had hired him in London before the war and had kept him on ever since. According to Baudouin, John would drive him into town, where they would sell poultry and eggs. To raise cash, she said, Moore put in a sawmill and brought in a crew from the Sierra Nevadas to operate it. But within a few months it was clear he couldn't pay them, and they left. Like the sawmill workers, most of Moore's servants quit when their paychecks first bounced and then stopped altogether. But, despite his penury, Moore somehow managed to keep a skeleton staff. I like to think these men stayed out of loyalty, but it was a matter of necessity for some. Times were tough, and three square meals and a roof over one's head wasn't such a bad deal. Baudouin was especially fond of a butler named Oscar who had worked in Casa Grande for many years. "He was a wonderful old fellow," she said. "He had saved all his money for many years for a trip back East to visit his family. The night before he was to leave, he died." This sad story seems of a piece with the fate of Rancho San Carlos.

The poultry, dairy, and cattle operations, supplemented by occasional venison and boar, provided ample food for everyone who lived on the ranch. Baudouin recalled that Moore had an excellent Italian chef who knew how to cook wild game. Fresh produce came from a large vegetable garden and an orchard. Baudouin said she often took vegetables to the sawmill workers, who would invariably respond, "Here comes Carol with that damn broccoli." There was always liquor in the house. The steady stream of visitors Moore had entertained at Rancho San Carlos during the 1920s had dwindled to a trickle, but my grandfather would have considered it unforgiveable not to offer a drink to anyone who came through his door.

The Carmel locals were intrigued by Moore's precipitous fall from grace. "He is living there bankrupt in hiding on that great estate—his wife's left him," Una Jeffers wrote to a friend in 1932. Moore stayed in touch with a few close friends, including the Jefferses. Like so many others who had known Moore, the couple viewed him with a mixture of awe, admiration, and mistrust. In a letter to Bennett Cerf, Una wrote, "George Gordon Moore—that omnipotent and mysterious person—I can't begin to tell you in one letter about him." To another friend, Una described Moore as "a strange shifty man with a certain power & evidence of events about him who tells rotten jokes every minute." Despite their ambivalent feelings about Moore, the Jefferses found him "quite amazingly interesting." He captivated their imagination with his outsized lust for life and his fantastic tales about his past, especially his adventures with Sir John French during the war. Moore told the Jefferses that his paternal grandfather was the estimable Earl of Drogheda and that Florida Manor, an impressive Irish country house, belonged to his mother's family. None of Moore's claims were true, but at this low point in his life he probably enjoyed pretending to have distinguished bloodlines, like his horses and hounds.

One of Moore's friends was a man with the intriguing name of Francis John Clarence Westenra Plantagenet Hastings, sixteenth Earl of Huntingdon, who had arrived in California in the winter of 1930. Hastings was an itinerant, adventure-seeking British artist who had come with his wife from Tahiti, where he had been working on a movie set. They were staying with their friend Gouverneur Morris, a pulp novelist, at his estate in Monterey. Hoping to tamp down his hard-partying lifestyle, Hastings was looking for a quiet place to live and get back to his painting. Morris sent him to see his old friend George Moore, who offered to rent the couple the cottage where Robert Louis Stevenson had recuperated in 1879. The Hastings soon acquainted themselves with the Carmel art scene. Una Jeffers wrote to a friend about having lunch at the cottage, prepared by "a Filipino cook who can roast a duck admirably."

The Jefferses occasionally took friends up to the ranch to meet Moore. One such visitor was Mabel Dodge Luhan, the writer and pioneering arts patron whose circle included Gertrude Stein, Alfred Stieglitz, and Georgia O'Keeffe. Mabel lived in Taos, New Mexico, with her fourth and final husband, Tony Luhan, a Taos Pueblo Indian. She ran a spiritually grounded salon of sorts in the adobe that she and Tony built, entertaining artists and writers including

D. H. Lawrence, whose work was considerably influenced by the time he spent there. On Mabel's first of several visits to the ranch, Moore insisted on giving her an Irish wolfhound that she had admired.

A couple of months following Moore's divorce from Esther in April 1933, the Jefferses visited him and were disturbed by the "desolation" they found at the ranch. But despite his low spirits Moore rallied in September to host his annual Labor Day barbecue. He called around to his friends, urging them to come. The Jefferses had house guests and declined the invitation. But Una later reported to Mabel that the event had been something of a disaster. "Heard afterward all the help got *drunk*," she wrote. "(It was Labor Day & all the help at the party! Ranch hands and cowboys etc.) a woman and child were killed when car tipped over." Moore went silent after that fiasco, causing Una to wonder whether he had abandoned the ranch.

The drained swimming pool, c. 1937

Moore occasionally emerged from his isolation to have lunch parties at the ranch with friends in Carmel who remained loyal or at least curious enough to make the trip. One such occasion took place when my mother and David were visiting their father. Moore summoned them from their beds and ordered them to go out and shoot some game birds. He told them that he had invited guests to lunch and wanted to serve them something special. The children were handy with guns and often hunted on the ranch. My mother even earned a "Marksman—First-Class" diploma from the National Rifle Association Junior Rifle Corps. They found a covey of quail in the underbrush and shot them on the ground. It was a memory my mother shared not with pride or satisfaction, but to illustrate her father's imperiousness. "It was not a sporting thing to do," she recalled. "But we had a job to do and we didn't have much time."

My mother with two mule deer and her rifle, c. 1935

My mother "riding" a boar, c. 1935

My mother gutting a boar while Moore's Irish wolfhounds wait for scraps, c. 1935

— CHAPTER 26 —

"My Easter Holidays"

IRONICALLY, it was after my grandparents' divorce that my grandfather began to spend time with his children. During the school year, Sheilah and David lived with Emma and their mother, but they spent summers and occasional holidays under Emma's care at Rancho San Carlos, where their father lived penniless and alone. My mother memorialized a visit over Easter vacation in 1936 in a little book that she made by hand. The book consists of twenty carefully typewritten pages, about five by eight inches in size, fastened at top and bottom by two brass pins. My mother was a bookish child, as the title page makes clear.

MY EASTER HOLIDAYS

A Story of Two Children and Their Nurse on an Easter Vacation

By Sheila Blair Moore

Copyrighted April 13, 1936. Hermit Copyrighting of the United States.

Insured 25¢. No part of this book may be copied for profit. Order of:

R.H.P.

My Easter Holiday's cover illustration by Sheila Blair Moore

I found this slim sheaf of papers in an old scrapbook of my mother's that was salvaged from the 1989 house fire. The brittle, browned pages, I discovered, held tantalizing clues about her early life. (As a girl, my mother often spelled her name "Sheila," rather than "Sheilah.") Unlike the dark stories my mother told later about her confusing and disrupted childhood, her contemporaneous account of a week at the ranch was cheerfully prosaic.

I wondered how my mother's memory had played with her experiences. How did she see her life and her family back then? Was there a point later on when she began to feel the pain of her broken family and her memories shifted in a minor key? Perhaps my mother's book revealed a fresher memory, one that was not warped by the sad history that was to follow.

In 1936, my mother was twelve and her father was sixty. In her book, she referred to him as "Daddy." Given his woeful shortcomings as a father, it's odd to think of him as anyone's Daddy. And yet in my mother's account, he comes across as a reasonable facsimile of a parent. He took the children on long horseback rides, sometimes to inspect his broodmares and their foals. He had the family's tennis rackets repaired so everyone could play, even though the court was crazed with cracks and crabgrass. One evening he planned an outing to Monterey to see the famous Tom Mix Circus. The children were eager to see the celebrated cowboy and his "Wonder Horse Tony," but the car's headlights weren't working, so they couldn't go.

David's recollection of these visits paints an even more poignant picture of my grandfather. Perhaps the hardship of his recent years had rendered him a kinder, more attentive father. In anticipation of the children's visit, he installed a ping-pong table at one end of the living room. He ate dinner with them every night, and afterwards they would sit around the fire in the living room talking and playing games. My mother and David had no trouble keeping themselves amused at the ranch. They built a hut in a dry riverbed. They rode into the hills to hunt wild cattle, penning them with a rope tied at

Hacienda living room, c. 1936

one end to a tree and at the other end to one of their horses' saddles. They visited the baby goats and the "chicken ranch." They made boats out of shingles and sailed them on the lake, eventually bombarding them with stones. There was a game of dare that involved climbing high into the rafters above the hayloft and jumping into piles of hay below. My mother and David seemed unusually close for a sister and brother in that typically antagonistic stage of sibling adolescence. But having grown up with so few friends their own age, they had to make do with each other. As David put it, "Sheilah was the only other kid around."

Although my grandfather had stopped handing out paychecks by this time, several cowboys worked on the ranch and lived in a bunkhouse. One day my mother reported that "Kim [the foreman] went down to Robinson's Canyon to get Shorty, Lasher, Jack, and Hard-At-It, who were fixing fences. Kim doesn't know what Hard-At-It's real name is and apparently no one does." It was not uncommon in those days

"My Easter Holidays"

for single men to show up at the ranch offering to work in exchange for bed and board.

I was surprised by the impression of my mother that comes across in "My Easter Holidays." In my experience, she had always been down-to-earth and unsentimental; I assumed that she had always been that way. But at age twelve, she wrote with the flowery cheer of a Victorian schoolgirl. One day's entry begins, "The morning dawned bright and sunny much to our pleasure." Describing a family tennis game, she wrote, "David is very good for the little tennis he has played." Where had she acquired such a treacly tone of voice? I found the answer in her book.

At one point during the visit, my mother wrote that she was struck with "a touch of that awful hay-fever" and spent the day in the house reading a book from a series about a girl named Elsie Dinsmore. "They're the only books of which I never tire," she wrote, adding, "it is odd, too, for most girls find them dull." I had never heard of Elsie Dinsmore and I was curious to find out what sort of books my mother was reading at that age. There were many popular books for girls back then including *The Secret Garden* and *Anne of Green Gables*, not to mention series such as the Nancy Drew books. My mother might have read these too, but during the spring of 1936, she was obsessed with Elsie Dinsmore. I thought that Elsie Dinsmore, whoever she was, might provide some insight into my mother's adolescent psyche.

Elsie Dinsmore was the creation of Martha Finley, a teacher, devout Christian, and prolific writer of Sunday school tracts. Born in Ohio in 1828 to a Presbyterian minister and his wife, Finley never married. *Elsie Dinsmore*, published in 1867, was a best-seller; the only children's book to sell more copies in the nineteenth century was Louisa May Alcott's *Little Women*.

When we first meet Elsie, she is, for all intents and purposes, an orphan. Her mother, we learn, died in childbirth. She has never met her father, who has been traveling in Europe for the eight years since his wife's death. She is forced to live with neglectful cousins. Already inured to a life of austere piety, Elsie consoles herself by praying for the day when her father will come home and shower her with love. But when her father returns, he subjects her to harsh discipline, which she accepts with slavish submission. After a joyous reconciliation they engage in daily bible reading accompanied by fervent displays of physical affection. A particularly cringe-worthy moment occurs the morning of Elsie's wedding day. "'My darling!' murmured the father, in low, half tremulous accents, putting his arm about the slender waist, 'my beautiful darling! how can I give you to another?' and again and again his lips were pressed to hers in long, passionate kisses."

What did Finley mean to suggest in this scene about the nature of Elsie's relationship with her father? Was Finley in love with her own father? Perhaps. But setting aside questions about the inner stirrings of an unmarried Sunday school teacher from Ohio, what could my mother possibly have seen in these sentimental, religiously freighted books? What was so intriguing to her about the story of a motherless girl in love with her cruel father? What does it say about her attitude toward her own parents that her favorite fictional character was a girl who had never known her mother and whose father was a dictatorial bully? Maybe Elsie Dinsmore had told me more than I wanted to know about my mother's early life.

"My Easter Holidays"

— CHAPTER 27 —

Orphans

MY MOTHER WASN'T AN ORPHAN, but she might as well have been. Her parents were distant and preoccupied. Although she and her brother were never starving or shoeless, their father's financial collapse was an icy plunge into the real world. My mother could never shake the frugal habits of her Depression childhood, and I bore the brunt of her fixation.

Whenever we met after I'd moved away from home, she couldn't keep herself from staring at my feet and saying, "*Another* new pair of shoes?" When I gave her a pretty nightgown for Christmas, she lamented, "But I don't *need* another nightgown." The last straw came when I was practicing law in New York and she came to the city for a brief visit. I met her for breakfast at the hotel where she was staying. She entered the dining room carrying a large shopping bag filled with clothing I had not worn since my high school days. "I thought you could use these," she said, setting the bag down by my chair. "They're perfectly good." I burst into tears. Was my mother deliberately tormenting me? Could she not accept that I had a career and a big enough salary to buy fashionable clothes? Did she disapprove of what she considered my excessive vanity? Maybe she was revisiting the precarious times of her Depression childhood, when only her detested mother spent money on stylish attire. Elsie Dinsmore, after all, was content with whatever hand-me-downs she received from her dismissive cousins.

My mother might easily have identified with the girl growing up in a broken home surrounded by unpredictable and tyrannical adults. Like Tom and Daisy Buchanan, my grandparents were heedless people who "smashed up things and creatures and then retreated back into their money or their vast carelessness." Although my mother always professed to abhor organized religion, perhaps back then she envied Elsie's unwavering faith in God. Living in a world of divorce, adultery, and alcohol, she might well have been drawn to Elsie's moral certainty. For Elsie, there was good and evil. In my mother's world, things were far less clear. Like Elsie, she had been raised to love and respect her elders, but how could she be expected to love and respect her parents when they were so negligent and preoccupied with their own problems? There was no telling when they would disappear from her life.

For my mother, life was a matter of "coping," a word she used often. It was a skill she had acquired early on. Her childhood was frequently disrupted by moves up and down the California coast to accommodate her mother's messy personal life. She learned to fend for herself as she navigated new homes, new schools, new neighborhoods. She said that she had changed schools so many times that she had the drill down perfectly. People paid no attention to her because they did not recognize her as a new girl. She prided herself on her self-sufficiency. In her eyes, asking for help was a cardinal sin, an admission of weakness. I had always assumed that she was simply stubborn in this regard. But I think she was too afraid to ask for help. If she couldn't trust her own parents to counsel and guide her, how could she trust anyone else? Such a lack of parental care left her deeply scarred. How could she help but pass along that emotional damage to me and my siblings?

When we were growing up, my father was too busy with work and his own recreational pastimes to spend much time with us. He left it to my mother to shepherd us through childhood and adolescence. I remember my early years as quite wonderful. There were lots of books, visits to art museums, summer trips to California, and overnight stays in the Blue Ridge Mountains. But our happy childhood came to an end when we reached adolescence. By that time, my mother was drinking too heavily to heed parental responsibilities. We learned to cope, just as she had. Neither she nor my father ever had our backs.

One episode stands out in my memory. When I was fourteen, I flew alone to Michigan to visit a friend at her family's summer house. I missed my connection in Chicago, and when I didn't get off the plane in Traverse City, my friend's mother was extremely worried. She called my mother, who responded, "Don't worry. I'm sure she'll turn up eventually." I did, of course, but my friend told me recently that her parents had always referred to me as "the orphan" on account of my parents' neglect.

My mother's benders seemed to come from nowhere. Sometimes she would call us out of our beds in the middle of the night and launch into a vague harangue about the farm. Once she called Jennie and me downstairs and told us to scrub the kitchen floor. We found her, as usual, bleary eyed and reeking of alcohol. Afraid to disobey her, we began collecting rags and a plastic bucket. After a while she seemed satisfied with our efforts and shambled back to her bedroom. We stayed awake for a long time that night talking about our mother. We were never safe from her rages.

Less dramatic but nonetheless disturbing, when she was drinking she often failed to do things she had agreed to, like picking us up at school or meeting us at the airport. Even worse, she would sometimes appear at events completely soused and make a display of herself. Shortly after Chris and I were married, my mother showed up uninvited and blind drunk at a lecture he was giving at the Folger Shakespeare Theatre in Washington, D.C. As she wove her way down the aisle, she announced in a loud voice, "That's my son-in-law." He was mortified but not surprised. He'd seen this behavior before.

We children also suffered on account of my mother's emotional austerity. She loathed sentimentality. Christmas was an annual nightmare. My mother hated the holiday, which to her smacked of phoniness and vulgarity. She relied on large quantities of booze, surreptitiously imbibed, to get through it. We knew for certain that my mother would behave badly, but we never knew how bad it was going to be. Sometimes she emerged from her bedroom on Christmas morning drunk and mean-spirited. She would rip open a few presents and disappear. One year she invited several people for Christmas Eve dinner, including a woman whom she had suspected of having an affair with my father. (I later learned that she was right.) Before stumbling off to bed, my mother brought out a lukewarm casserole of hamburger, tomato soup, and macaroni, something akin to the school cafeteria staple called "American Chop Suey." It was her way of giving us all the finger. My father tried to pretend that nothing was wrong, even after a few guests fished random pieces of cutlery out of the dish. My siblings and I could only laugh. It was how we coped with my mother's irascible, unpredictable behavior.

My mother's emotional austerity carried over into her treatment of our animals. As much as she loved them, she had no qualms about putting them down when they had outlived their useful purpose. One grim winter day she decided that her beloved foxhunter Siggy's time had come. After slugging down half a bottle of vodka, she rode him to the hunt kennels where he was to be slaughtered and fed to the hounds. She ordered me and my sister to drive to the kennels and bring her home. We were horrified, but we did it. As my mother had said when she told the story of shooting the game birds, "We had a job to do."

Strangely enough, we never confronted my mother about her horrible drunken behavior. We were afraid of what she might say or do if we were to raise the subject of her drinking. We did our best to forget the unpleasantness and move on. It was safer to let that sleeping dog lie.

My son Tommy was born five months after my parents' house fire in 1989. My parents came to New York to celebrate the arrival of their first grandchild. It was a difficult birth, and I stayed in the hospital for nearly a week. My mother spent time with Chris during my recuperation and talked a lot about the fire, which had not only destroyed many of the family's possessions but had taken the lives of her two dogs. She insisted that the fire shouldn't have troubled her so much. After all, she explained to Chris, she had suffered so many losses in her life that she should have been accustomed to them by then. She talked about the loss of Rancho San Carlos and how much that place had meant to her. She described how her mother had summarily swept her father and stepfather Roark out of her life. She talked about how Jennie had "given away" her irreplaceable jewelry. She had lost many beloved animals, some due to sheer carelessness. Her parents had forced her to cope and she had finely honed that skill. Denying herself the right to mourn was just her way of coping with terrible losses. But the losses stayed with her and instilled bitterness in her heart that spewed out whenever she opened a bottle.

For all my mother's shortcomings, she was wonderful when she was sober. My siblings and I appreciated that she was much hipper than other mothers we knew. She had a sharp tongue and an eagle eye for phoniness and pretension. She liked edgy writers like Nabokov, Mailer, and Henry Miller and encouraged us to read them. She listened to recordings of cowboy singers like Marty Robbins and Hank Williams. She had never forgiven her mother for refusing to let her go to a concert by Bob Wills and the Texas Playboys in San Francisco. She dutifully accompanied my father to the symphony and the opera, but she preferred Elvis Presley. She bought the Beatles' first album, "Meet the Beatles," as soon as it was released in January 1964. A lifelong smoker, she showed us how to do the twist by putting out a cigarette under her foot. When I was in boarding school in Massachusetts, she sent me cartons of cigarettes in the mail because they were so much cheaper in Virginia. My father told her that mailing cigarettes interstate was illegal, but she went on doing it. "Do you know how expensive cigarettes are up there?" she asked him.

My mother was unfathomable till the end. In the eyes of the world, she led an enviable life. She was married to a successful lawyer, her mother was an heiress, and her father was a legend in his time. She always seemed to view her situation with irony; she knew that appearances were deceiving. She had ultimately seen her father as an imposter, an outsider trying to be an insider. Perhaps she identified with that sense of not belonging. Growing up, she had experienced life in a way that set her apart from the other women in her circle. It was clear from the way she talked about them that she disdained them for what she saw as a facile acceptance of their privileged, unexamined lives.

Unlike Elsie Dinsmore, my mother never said much about her feelings for her father. She acknowledged how emotionally distant he had been as a parent. She once commented on her father's formality in signing his early letters to her "George Gordon Moore" rather than something more familiar. In my father's law files, I found a letter my grandfather had written to her on December 21, 1962, when he was once again hoping to make money on a mining scheme.

> Sheilah, darling, I want you to know that you are the one in my life of whom I have always been proud. When only about four, on old Roany you drove in the broodmares, scaring the day lights out of tough old Henry Dunn, who came complaining to me. When Feen Darling couldn't brand the polo foals, until you were to come home and identify the thoroughbred foals and separate; when about ten years old you could draw a horse's head so that even another horse would recognize it—& so many more until you became the best cowboy on the ranch & later, when you grew up, you had the good sense to pick Henry for a husband. As for myself I hope you may not be disappointed in me as a father. I am still unusually healthy and if I can keep it, you will see that I will win out.
> All my love to you and yours, Father

The letter baffled me. Was he finally expressing paternal feelings that he had never shared, or was he just trying to loosen her purse strings? Maybe both. How did my mother react when she read this letter? Did it wrench her heart to revisit memories of happy times on the ranch? This outpouring of feelings was not enough to erase the disappointment and trouble her father had caused her over the years, but I think it softened her.

As ambivalent as my mother was about her father, she was unequivocally contemptuous of her mother. I cannot remember a single nice thing my mother ever said about her. She depicted her as a selfish, narcissistic drunk who carted her children around with no regard for their wishes or well-being. She told us about her mother's attempt to sabotage her courtship with my father. My parents had met on a blind date at the racetrack in Charlestown, West Virginia. My father was attending law school at the University of Virginia; my mother was attending Sweet Briar College, a girls finishing school in Virginia that was the only place Esther would permit her to go, although she had been admitted to Stanford and Berkeley. Esther was not pleased to hear that my mother was dating a law student from Elmira, New York, who had no social distinction. At one point Esther learned that my mother was spending a few days in Charlottesville visiting her beau. She was furious and summoned her to come to New York immediately, insisting that her presence was required at some fancy social occasion. Thoroughly fed up with Esther's unreasonable demands, she replied, "Oh balls, mother," and hung up the phone.

My mother also disdained Esther for her ignorance of practical things. Although she could sit comfortably on a horse, she didn't have any idea how to care for one. Everything was appearance, details be damned. One day when her cook was sick, Esther attempted to prepare a meal from a cookbook. She did not know what an egg yolk was, and assumed it to be the white part, because it went around the yellow, like the yoke of an ox. The meal could not have been a success.

CHAPTER 28

Out Stealing Horses

In January 1939, with the ink barely dry on the Roark divorce decree, Esther married for the fourth time. Her new husband, Sidney Webster Fish, had been a good friend of hers and Moore's. Fish's first wife, Olga, who had also been a close friend of the Moores, had died of cancer a couple of years earlier at age forty-seven. The wedding ceremony was an intimate gathering in the living room at the Fish Ranch, just a few miles as the crow flies from Moore's sadly empty Casa Grande. It had been nearly five years to the day since my grandmother had tied the knot with Aidan Roark in that same room, with the blessing of Olga and Sidney. My mother and David had recently settled into their new home at the Fish Ranch and were among the handful of people present to witness their mother's latest romantic foray. By then, Esther's turbulent marital history was notorious. Before the wedding, the *San Francisco Examiner* reported that "another distinguished surname is soon to be added to the string of distinguished surnames of Mrs. Esther Foss Moore Roark. But what that surname will be came as a distinct surprise to all but the best informed circles of West Coast society. The name will be Fish, which is the name of the wealthy Carmel Valley 'rancher,' Sidney Fish, member of the same old Knickerbocker family that produced Representative Hamilton Fish, a cousin."

Of the dozen or so newspapers that reported the marriage, all but one referred to it as Esther's *third* marriage, citing only her previous marriages to George Moore and Aidan Roark. Esther and her family had succeeded in sweeping her marriage to Albert Hickman into the dustbin of social history. But people in Boston knew the whole story. The *Boston Globe* announced "'FOSS TWIN' WILL WED FOURTH TIME." The subhead read: "Daughter of Ex-Governor Will Marry Mine Owner—Divorced Year Ago from Aidan Roark." The article featured a large photograph of forty-four-year-old Esther looking haggard and hungover.

Unlike George Moore and Aidan Roark, Sidney Fish came from Old Money. He happened to own some mining interests, but he had also inherited a substantial fortune. The Great Depression slowed his cash flow but it did not put a dent in his lifestyle. Just up the Carmel Valley, meanwhile, Moore continued to live in impoverished seclusion. What did he think when he learned that Esther, who had already humiliated him by running off with a handsome young polo star, was marrying his neighbor, Sidney Fish, an ironclad American aristocrat? Did he have the same poisonous feelings of envy and resentment that F. Scott Fitzgerald had, knowing that he was born on the wrong side of the social divide? As he reflected on his glory days at Rancho San Carlos, did my grandfather seethe at the unfairness of life?

At this point, Esther did everything she could to sever any ties David still had with his father. She and Sidney Fish set up a guardianship for David naming Sidney as guardian. When David was sixteen, she decided that his middle name should be changed from Gordon to Sturtevant, after her maternal grandfather. I suppose she meant this to be the final expungement of George Gordon Moore from her son's life. Esther apparently cared less about my mother's relationship with her father. It doesn't appear that any guardianship was established for her. Nor was her middle name, Blair—after Moore's mother, Ruth Blair—ever changed.

I have no idea how my mother felt about this disparate treatment. She must have known about David's name change, if not about the guardianship. But she never mentioned it, nor did David tell his children about it. Like so many of my family's secrets, I only learned about these arrangements by chance, when Diana Fish, Stuyvie's widow, called me to tell me she'd discovered the information in some legal documents she found when going through old family papers at the Fish Ranch, where she still lives.

Regardless of how Moore felt about Esther's marriage to Sidney, Esther and Sidney seemed to have no qualms about Moore's lurking presence in Carmel Valley. Una Jeffers found this lack of sentiment peculiar. She wrote to a friend, "You know the Moore and Fish ranches—great domains march side by side back into the mountains here. Not long ago Robin and I and those two [Sidney and Esther] rode into Sidney's back ranch for the day. . . . Everything did seem queer—to see those two riding quietly and with no apparent feeling of strangeness over property once George Moore's and looking down over territory which must have been packed with queer terrible memories of one kind or another for her. Here she had spent years with that powerful, clever, wicked man, here her children had spent their childhood." I don't know what "queer terrible memories" of Rancho San Carlos might have lingered in Esther's mind, but Una Jeffers had been intimately acquainted with the goings-on there, and perhaps there were ghastly stories to be told.

On a cool January morning in 1940, my mother and David set out from Rancho San Carlos on horseback, leading a string of twelve horses tied head to tail. As David later told me, they were taking the remaining few horses from the San Carlos to the Fish Ranch. All the others, Thoroughbred stallions and mares, polo ponies, and cattle horses, had been sold off earlier to pay my grandfather's debts. David told me about an auction that had taken place on the ranch while he and my mother were visiting. They had not been told about the sale and were deeply disturbed to see the horses being trotted out one by one for the auctioneer's call and then loaded onto trucks and driven away.

When David and my mother made their final departure from Rancho San Carlos that morning, they were not certain what was going to happen to the place. Their father had disappeared a few weeks earlier. They had spent the previous several days helping Emma and John take the remaining furniture from Casa Grande to the Fish Ranch on John's old poultry truck. They knew that their father had lost all his money. But they did not know that he had failed to pay the mortgage on the ranch—approximately $160,000—causing the bank to foreclose on the property. Their mother had told them nothing. She considered it vulgar to discuss personal matters, particularly those involving marriage or money. But they knew it would likely be the last time they'd set foot on the ranch where they had spent their childhood.

My mother led the procession on a handsome chestnut gelding called Nibbler. David, on his fat old mare, Peaches, brought up the rear. Suddenly they heard the rumble of a vehicle far off in the distance, and seconds later they could make out the Monterey County sheriff's black van creeping slowly up the driveway toward the house. They'd seen the van often at the ranch in the previous weeks and they knew it meant trouble. If the sheriff saw them he would seize all the horses, including the two they were riding. The children knew the terrain well and hurried their convoy down a rocky path into a canyon, safely shielded from the road. My mother dismounted and watched the road. Minutes passed. They waited anxiously, hoping that the horses wouldn't jostle each other or let out a whinny that might draw the sheriff's attention. Finally the van passed from view. They knew the sheriff would be busy the rest of the morning searching the house and barns for anything of value that had been left behind. They also knew he would find nothing. After waiting a few more minutes, they resumed their journey.

Three hours later, my mother and David reached their destination. They were greeted by Emma and an amiable young cowboy who ran the Fish Ranch's cattle operation. The children were weary but nonetheless thoroughly satisfied with themselves. They couldn't wait to tell Emma about ducking the sheriff. It never crossed their minds that, as far as he was concerned, they were common horse thieves.

After their felonious departure from Rancho San Carlos, Sheilah and David's lives settled into stability with Esther's marriage to Sidney Fish. The children had been moving in and out of different schools since their parents' divorce in 1933, making and losing friends along the way. Back in Carmel, my mother attended a local private school and led a relatively normal teenage life. During the summer, she and David rode horses and worked cattle on the Fish Ranch. Emma continued to live with the family. Stuyvie Fish, a year older than my mother, became one of her closest friends. Although they never saw eye-to-eye politically, they always remained on good terms. In 1965, he asked my mother to co-host a luncheon at the ranch in honor of Princess Margaret and Lord Tony Snowden during their infamous trip to the United States. The menu included barbecued wild boar raised on the ranch.

Perhaps Sidney Fish and my grandmother were drawn together by their common predilection for alcohol. Excessive drinking was a constant at the Fish Ranch. My mother spoke of one particularly unpleasant alcohol-infused episode there. It occurred on my parents' wedding day, December 29, 1948. They were married in the living room at the Fish Ranch, the same place where my grandmother had married Aidan Roark in 1936 and Sidney Fish in 1939. My parents' wedding party included my father's extremely proper mother and sister, who had flown with my father from Elmira, New York, for the occasion.

My parents' courtship had been brief. They had met only a few times prior to their engagement. A few years before my mother died she intimated that she had married my father out of necessity, convinced by her mother that she was running out of time to find a husband. My mother told me that she did not recognize my father when he got off the plane from New York. "He was wearing a raincoat and had just gotten his hair cut," she said by way of explanation. It was the first time my mother had met her mother-in-law (my paternal grandfather had died several years earlier), and the mutual disapproval was palpable.

George Moore was not invited to his daughter's wedding, although he could easily have made the trip from Los Angeles. Instead, my mother was given away by Sidney Fish, who was so drunk my mother had to practically carry him from one end of the living room to the other. After the ceremony, Sidney was supposed to drive the wedding party from the ranch to the reception at the Cypress Point Club in Pebble Beach. But when the time came, it was clear to my mother and everyone else that he was in no condition to drive. My mother was mortified. How was she to cope? She picked up the train of her long-sleeved velvet wedding gown, snatched the car keys from her stumbling stepfather, and ushered the astonished group out to Sidney's black Packard sedan, which was parked by the door. She arranged herself and her gown in the driver's seat and drove everyone to the club for the reception.

My parents on their wedding day, December 29, 1948

In Julian Graham's wedding photographs, my mother's expression ranges from dazed to miserable. Even when she managed a smile while sipping champagne with my father, she looked grim. She might as well have been at her own funeral. Esther and Sidney were too drunk to attend the reception. Sidney died a year later, a month shy of his sixty-fifth birthday. The newspapers reported simply that he "succumbed in his sleep" but everyone knew he had drunk himself to death.

Esther and Sidney Fish, c. 1947

The bottle eventually caught up with Esther, too. On November 26, 1954, her maid discovered her dead in her bedroom at the Palo Corona Ranch. She was sixty years old. Her obituary stated that she had been in poor health but that her death was unexpected. No cause of death was given. My mother made a quick trip out to California to attend the funeral. By then my parents had settled in Washington, D.C. My father had just made partner in a law firm, and my mother had her hands full with Gordon and Jennie, both under the age of three. Years later, when Chris asked my mother how Esther had died, she mimed a drinker holding a bottle in her hand and pouring its contents into her open mouth.

— CHAPTER 29 —

Ending Up

IN 1963, LONG AFTER he had lost his fortune, my grandfather wrote a letter to his old friend Averell Harriman congratulating him on making the cover of *Time* magazine. As a senior State Department official, Harriman had just succeeded in negotiating the Partial Nuclear Test Ban Treaty with Russia. Reminiscing about their early years, my grandfather wrote that "what they now call the roaring twenties was ours. It is my private conceit that in those years our little coterie had the greatest robust fun, the highest joy with the true zest of living without injury to anyone in that era." The coterie, which my grandfather sometimes referred to as their "closely held corporation," included Tommy Hitchcock and a few other close friends. Continuing in the same nostalgic vein, Moore listed the places where they'd had their fun. "Our habitat on the Bay at Sands Point with open house, polo at Meadow Brook from May until October, your duck shooting at Arden [Harriman's estate in Orange County, New York], and 44 East 52nd Street in the off season. Winters and wild boar hunting at my ranch at Carmel, California, and polo from Del Monte to Pasadena."

Moore was staking his claim to the glittering epoch that F. Scott Fitzgerald had labeled the Jazz Age. I don't know if my grandfather ever read *The Great Gatsby*, but his recollection of having "the highest joy with the true zest of living" could have been penned by Fitzgerald himself. If Moore had read the novel, I don't know if he would have seen himself in the Gatsby role. David surmised that he would have been furious to be cast as a hopeless wannabe like Gatsby. "He wanted to be *part* of that society," said David, "not a *parody* of it."

While Averell Harriman rode the crest of the wave from the 1920s onward, the intervening years had not been so triumphant for Moore. Just before the Rancho San Carlos foreclosure in 1940, he had fled Carmel for Los Angeles, dodging creditors and the scorn of friends and family who had once held him in high regard. He rented a modest two-bedroom apartment near Hollywood Boulevard where he lived with his valet, John Raming, who continued to work for him until old age forced him into retirement in the early 1950s. Once settled in Los Angeles, Moore again began tracking the mineral markets, determined to regain his fortune. Throughout the '40s and '50s, Moore somehow managed to keep the wolf from the door, but he struck no goldmines, literally or otherwise. Ventures that started with promise usually fizzled. But, as David said, "He loved the thrill of the chase." Around 1960, he acquired mineral interests on 150 acres in the Mojave Desert, which he believed to be rich in tungsten, gold, and iron ore. He was certain his luck had finally changed.

The Russians had recently sent cosmonaut Yuri Gagarin into orbit around the earth, taking a commanding lead in the space race and humiliating the United States. On May 25, 1961, President John F. Kennedy appeared before Congress to ask for several billion additional dollars for the country's nascent space program so that America could reestablish its primacy over its Cold War enemy. NASA kicked into high gear, amping up the demand for tungsten. With its extremely high melting point and tensile strength, tungsten was the ideal material for coating rockets and missiles to prevent them from burning up when they reentered the earth's atmosphere.

The tungsten market was suddenly hot, and Moore was ready to cash in. But he needed money. To raise capital for this venture Moore incorporated two stock companies, Metals and Minerals Corporation and Atolia Tungsten. He hired a mineralogist who determined that the property was, indeed, rich in tungsten. He assembled a group of potential investors and worked up plans to build a processing plant. He promised David and my parents that, if they invested in his operation, he would soon be able to fulfill his "final ambition." As he wrote to my father, his wish was "to have you and Sheilah furnished with a racing establishment as good as my old friend, Sonny Whitney, and have David take a first-class polo team to play in England." Tungsten was the golden ring and it seemed to be within my grandfather's reach.

In 1962, China was the leading producer of tungsten and controlled the world market. Just as Moore was preparing to mine domestic tungsten, China flooded the market and the price dropped to practically nothing. As Moore explained in a letter to his friend John L. Lewis, longtime president of the United Mine Workers, "the entire U.S. tungsten industry caved in. Even Union Carbide put its production into inventory." But he was unwilling to admit defeat. Indomitable as ever, he told Lewis: "I had a H— of a time to keep the ship afloat, but finally survived."

My parents and David did their best to plug holes in Moore's leaky vessel. Letters in my father's legal files reflect their efforts to stabilize his precarious business affairs. There were lawsuits against him for fraud, as there had been in the past. One such case involved a man who claimed to have made a "short term investment" with Moore. He sued when the promised return failed to materialize as forecast. Moore's response to the lawsuit was, "Well, that poor bastard is one permanent investor now." Lawsuits like this ran aground when it became clear that Moore had no assets to satisfy a judgment against him.

Moore remained hopeful till the end. "He didn't get down in the mouth about it," said David. "He truly believed he was going to do it again. He could talk the money right out of Fort Knox." Whenever he made any money, he spent it. At one point, a silver mine netted him several thousand dollars. The first thing he did was to buy a second-hand Lincoln and hire a chauffeur. David and my mother urged him to put the money into a savings account. But he refused. "You can have the damned money," he told David. "Just leave me twenty bucks for pills. Because I can't live that way."

My father once told a story about chiding his father-in-law for putting together deals that were patently illegal. My grandfather's response was, "Who's going to send an eighty-six-year-old man to jail?" In the spring of 1961, he got an answer to that question. He was arrested and put in jail in Barstow, California, a town in the western Mojave Desert. He was charged with failing to pay the employees of his Metals and Minerals Corporation, in violation of the state labor code. He was given a six-month suspended sentence and released on probation on the condition that he make good on his payroll obligations.

In March 1962, Moore was arrested again for failing to pay the state the employment taxes he had withheld from his employees. On hearing this news, David reluctantly headed to Los Angeles and hired a lawyer named Alfred C. Phillips to negotiate a plan with the state tax authority. After seeing Moore, David reported to my parents. "Father seems in very low spirits," he wrote. "No wonder! However, he says he would rather go to jail than to dissolve the companies to pay off the debts. And believe it or not, throughout all our conversations he keeps referring to the need of a slightly new type of plant! Christ!"

Several years later, my father received a letter from Phillips. "We enjoyed working with you and David," he wrote, "and I personally greatly appreciated the opportunity of becoming acquainted with George Gordon Moore who, as you described in one of your letters, is 'a fantastic person.'" As I read this letter, I paused to consider the word "fantastic" and its various meanings. Fantastic can mean exceptionally good. But I think my father and Phillips used the word in its more literal sense, as *Collier's Dictionary* defines it: "a lack of restraint of imagination, suggesting that which is extravagantly fanciful or unreal in design, conception, or construction."

In 1964, Moore revived his tungsten plans. Forever hopeful, he contacted his old friend Peggy Hitchcock and learned that her son Billy had taken over his father's partnership position at Lehman Brothers. (Tommy Hitchcock died in England in 1944 when a fighter plane he was testing crashed.) In a letter to my father, Moore wrote, "I think I told you that Tommy Hitchcock's son, Wm. Mellon Hitchcock, is now a partner in Lehman Bros. And I would like to offer this firm our certificates. I have an invitation to stay with his mother on Long Island when I next go to New York." Moore persuaded Billy, who happened to be in Los Angeles on business, to check out the Mojave mining site. Evidently, Billy was sufficiently impressed to return a few weeks later with a geologist to drill some test holes to assess the amount of tungsten available. Moore was confident that there was enough to net at least thirty million dollars in profit. Emboldened by young Hitchcock's interest, Moore directed my father to register stock in Atolia Tungsten with the Securities and Exchange Commission, sales of which were to raise the three million dollars necessary to fund the mining and processing operation. "Surely with this kind of a showing money should be available," Moore assured him, adding that "my two sources here promised, but have not yet functioned." Various legal complications ensued, the "sources" ultimately failed to "function," and the plan went nowhere.

At the age of ninety-one, Moore was yet again in dire straits. With two failed tungsten deals behind him, he upped the ante, pinning his hopes on gold. In spring 1967, he wrote a letter to Harold James, Chief of the U.S. Geological Survey in Washington, D.C. "Western newspapers report that your dept is conducting an investigation to discover undeveloped potential gold areas," he began. "We believe that two corporations, the control of which are owned by myself and family, located at Red Mountain, on Highway 395, San Bernardino, California, own mineral deposits containing the gold for which you are looking." Like Moore's string of prospective investors, James did not go for the bait.

During his final years, my grandfather was too frail to travel east at Christmas. But he continued to shower my siblings and me with mind-improving literature. Several weeks before Christmas in 1968, he wrote to my mother asking her to buy us a volume of Lord Thomas Babington Macaulay's essays. As he explained, "the essay on Milton, I think, is the best essay in the English language." Curious to see what my grandfather had found so extraordinary in the essay, I tracked down the collection of essays. It's an erudite discussion of the art of poetry and the Civil War that took place during Milton's life in seventeenth-century England. Macaulay wrote at length about the "truth of madness" that underlay Milton's creative process. Did my grandfather see himself when he read "the strength of his imagination triumphed over every obstacle"?

The love of my grandfather's life may have been Diana Manners Cooper, but he ended up with a beautiful Russian woman who called herself Countess Sonia. "She was no more a countess than I'm a king," said David, "but she stayed with him and behind him." Countess Sonia, born Sophia Sonia Belikovich, had been a member of a celebrated vaudeville dance act and was part of Hollywood's Russian colony, a group of expatriates that included musicians and artists. As vaudeville waned in the early 1930s, Sonia tried her hand at the movies. Aside from a few bit parts in early talkies, she couldn't get her foot in the door. Seeing a dim future in Hollywood, she took her talents into the hospitality field, running a popular restaurant and nightclub with a bordello on the side. My grandfather frequented all three establishments. At age eighty-six, he boasted to David and my parents that he had contracted "the clap." I suppose he wanted them to know that no matter how badly he had failed in other areas of his life, he was still a ladies' man. David told me that whenever he visited his father, the old man would offer to fix him up with one of Sonia's "dancing girls." David would decline, telling his father, "She might look good to you, Daddy, but she's too old for me."

My grandfather and "Countess" Sonia celebrating his 93rd birthday, 1969

My grandfather referred to Sonia as his girlfriend. She was several years younger than him, and she must have enjoyed his company. She certainly didn't stay with him for his money. She shopped for him and kept him stocked with Zane Grey novels and the *Daily Racing Form*. According to David, he read constantly and quickly, sometimes delving into treatises on engineering and mining, which he read with a magnifying glass. My grandfather sent my parents a color photograph of Sonia and himself at his ninetieth birthday party in 1966. They look happy and celebratory, she in a sparkly floral gown, he in black tie sporting a red carnation in his lapel.

On May 16, 1971, Sonia found my grandfather dead in his bathroom. He had suffered a massive heart attack. As on so many occasions in his long and colorful life, he had been getting ready for a party.

— CHAPTER 30 —

Rancho San Carlos Revisited

ALTHOUGH OUR FAMILY spent several summers out in Carmel when I was young, we never visited Rancho San Carlos. My mother took us hiking at Big Sur and Point Lobos, and to the Salinas Rodeo, where she had competed as a teenager in calf roping and barrel racing. We visited old friends of hers in Pebble Beach and Monterey. But Rancho San Carlos was never mentioned, although I now realize we must have driven past it many times. In the summer of 2009, I went back to Carmel. While so much of my grandfather's life was irretrievably lost, Rancho San Carlos was something that physically remained. I wanted to see its mountains and grasslands, Casa Grande, and whatever else was left from my grandfather's glory years.

After the bank foreclosure in 1940, Rancho San Carlos had been purchased by a wealthy businessman named Arthur C. Oppenheimer and his cousin, Alice J. Rosenberg. Oppenheimer noted that "It was the game refuge that took my eye. I am a hunter and I am told it is one of the finest in this state." The family used the ranch as a vacation retreat and ran a cattle operation there. In the late 1960s, the ranch was used as the setting for the television western series *Lancer*. A scene from Woody Allen's *Sleeper* was also filmed there in 1973. When the ranch was put on the market in the late 1980s, local conservationists feared that the land would be subdivided, ruining its pristine beauty, wildlife, and water resources. A couple of real estate entrepreneurs worked out a compromise with the state that allowed them to sell up to 300 home sites ranging in size from several acres to several hundred while keeping the remainder undeveloped in perpetuity. The new owners renamed the ranch the Santa Lucia Preserve, dropping the Rancho San Carlos name that the property had carried since the early 1800s.

When I arrived in Carmel, I telephoned the organization that manages the property. The woman who answered the phone told me curtly that the Preserve was not open for public tours. When I explained that I was a granddaughter of George Gordon Moore, she immediately changed her tone and invited me to come for a visit. I arranged an appointment, and the next afternoon I arrived at the visitors center, a newly built stone structure adjacent to the closed iron gates just off the main road. The weather in the town of Carmel had been cool and overcast, but out in the valley, just three miles inland, it was hot and sunny. The air-conditioned offices were tastefully appointed with heavy wooden furniture and abundant fresh flowers. Tidy stacks of sales brochures were displayed on low coffee tables. A young sales agent named John, crisp and clean-cut as a Marine, greeted me with a confident handshake and explained that he would be showing me around the Preserve. He handed me a sheaf of literature and a bottle of chilled spring water. We climbed into his gleaming black Ford Explorer, a security guard unlocked the gates for us, and we began our journey up the circuitous driveway my mother had traveled so often in her father's Lincoln Continental.

What struck me first about the ranch was the sheer size of it. The figure of 23,000 acres was fixed in my mind but the number did not register with me until I actually set foot on the property. John told me that it was one-and-a-half times the size of Manhattan. As we drove along through miles of sun-gold meadows dotted with lupines and stands of oak and piñon trees, I thought about a taxi ride from Battery

Park to the Bronx and beyond. Suddenly the vista opened to the fog-shrouded Monterey Bay far below. John pulled over so I could take in the view. Before me was the Pacific coastline; behind me, hills rose in tiers to the distant horizon capped by the dark, undulating skyline of the Santa Lucia Range. Crickets thrummed in the grass. The air smelled of piñon and eucalyptus. A few deer grazed off in the distance. I imagined my mother and David loping along the ridges on their cowponies, perhaps the first people since the Esselen, an Indian tribe whose ancient homeland was the Santa Lucia Mountains, to have traversed those routes.

John had only recently arrived from Texas, and he knew less about the property than I did. His recitation of facts and figures was studded with stories about the ranch and my grandfather's life. He told me, for example, that my grandfather had been the bastard son of British royalty. I couldn't help but interject an occasional correction. Although John knew that I was there to explore my grandfather's past, he kept up his salesman's banter, as if he might talk me into a sale. Perhaps he hadn't yet heard the story about my grandfather losing the ranch. He pointed out some of the newly built homes, sprawling Spanish-style McMansions that mimicked Casa Grande, but on steroids. "Fourteen-thousand square feet," he said, slowing down to point out one gigantic house still under construction. "Eight million dollars," he added, nodding to another just down the road. He quoted the prices for available homesites we passed: 1.5 million; 2.2 million. I laughingly told him those were a bit out of my price range, trying to sound upbeat as the dollar signs crashed around in my head. John seemed unaware of the unseemliness of his suggestion that I might wish to buy back a sliver of the property that had once belonged to my family.

I wondered how my mother would have felt about this new incarnation of Rancho San Carlos. On the one hand, she had loved the ranch and would have been grateful that so much of the property had been left untouched. The ownership group has worked hard to maintain the pristine beauty of the land and to keep alive the ranch's history, which began long before my grandfather took possession of it. On the other hand, I imagined she would have sneered at the vulgarity of the new inhabitants in their multimillion-dollar houses. But back in the 1920s, her father's extravagant aspirations had not been so different.

Our first stop was the swimming complex, located within what had once been my grandfather's enormous polo barn. His other horse barns were gone, but the developers had preserved the polo barn's horseshoe-shaped structure and refurbished its fifty-plus stalls to house dressing rooms, a canteen, and other amenities. Some of the original stall doors had been saved as evidence of the building's former occupants. I could imagine my grandfather and his teammates slouching over their mallets in the doorway while polo ponies dozed in their stalls. John led me through an archway onto the sun-filled poolside terrace. The air was filled with the summery smells of chlorine, coconut oil, and grilled hamburgers. Bronzed boys in baggy surfer shorts executed cannonballs off the diving board and torpedoed headfirst down the giant water slide while girls watched and giggled. Young mothers, slim and tanned, splashed with tow-headed toddlers in the pool's shallow end. My grandfather's polo kingdom was gone, replaced by Ralph Lauren's Polo lifestyle.

We headed back to the Explorer to continue the tour. John drove on through the property, pointing out the new eighteen-hole golf course designed by the legendary Tom Fazio. John told me that when Fazio first saw the 350-acre site, he said, "You really don't need me. The course is already here." Moore would no doubt have declined a round of golf in favor of a day playing polo or hunting wild boar. But he appreciated quality and craftsmanship, and I supposed he would have approved of the course, so snugly nestled into the hills and natural vegetation that it seemed a part of the landscape he'd once cherished.

Twenty minutes later, we arrived at the ranch's most sacred precinct, the Redwood Grove, which John explained was a popular site for family celebrations and musical productions. We walked down the needle-strewn path into the grove. Sun filtered through the towering branches, creating delicious pockets of warmth in the cool, moist air. I stepped across the remnants of the gigantic, long-abandoned cement barbecue pit I'd seen in Arnold Genthe's haunting photographs. I pictured the chefs in their white toques tending the fire under the long metal spits that held whole wild boar and sides of ranch-raised beef. I could almost smell the smoky odor of seared meat. I imagined starlets and their suitors dancing the Charleston to the music of a jazz orchestra brought in from San Francisco. I could almost hear the tipsy laughter of guests, drunk on Prohibition booze. I got dizzy looking up to the cloudless blue sky through the same branches that had once stood watch over these rustic soirées. The sight of a cluster of Porta-Potties at the edge of the grove brought the curtain down on my reverie. They looked like blue mushrooms under the towering trees. John explained that they were left over from a wedding that had taken place in the grove the preceding weekend. It seemed to me a violation of my grandfather's legacy that Rancho San Carlos was now home to a Rent-a-Redwood Grove.

Our final stop was Casa Grande, which now serves as the Preserve's clubhouse. John assured me that it had been carefully restored to represent my grandfather's era. As with everything else at the ranch, the house and its accoutrements seemed larger than life. The front hall was decked with maps, photographs, and a menacing boar's head complete with fearsome tusks and tiny pig eyes. I wondered if it was the same one that had greeted Diana Manners Cooper back in 1927. The living room was furnished with leather sofas and club chairs modeled on photographs of the room taken when my grandfather lived there. The old ping-pong table, of course, was nowhere to be seen. The original stone fireplace, big enough to roast a boar, occupied one side of the room. On the opposite wall, the same French doors opened onto a terrace, but the swimming pool I'd seen in photographs was gone. John showed me the secret door that led to the basement, where my grandfather had hidden the generous store of wine and spirits he served to so many thirsty guests. Upstairs were eight guest rooms and the separate wing where my mother and David had lived with Emma. Each room bears the name of an original occupant or owner of the ranch from its earliest days. Because some of the weekend wedding guests were still staying in the hacienda, I was not permitted to look inside the rooms. John secured special dispensation to show me into the George Gordon Moore Room, which is said to have been my grandfather's own bedroom.

Moore had directed his architect to lay out the bedrooms so that each had an exquisite view of the ranch. Looking out the west-facing windows onto the hills and valleys that my grandfather had wakened to every morning, I realized how numb I had become during the previous three hours I'd spent touring the ranch. "Some view, huh?" said John. I nodded and tried to look cheerful. But inwardly I was experiencing the devastation my grandfather must have felt at losing this awesome piece of land and everything he had created here. I imagined his ambivalence at rejecting the offer of his fickle ex-wife to give him the money to pay off the mortgage and keep the property. After losing Esther to Aidan Roark and then suffering the indignity of her subsequent marriage to his neighbor and erstwhile friend Sidney Fish, accepting her largesse must have exceeded his capacity for humiliation. All he had left was his pride. What must have gone through his mind when he left Casa Grande for the last time and headed down the coast toward Los Angeles? Rancho San Carlos was the apotheosis of his dreams. But in the end it had vanished, as all dreams do.

Back at the visitors center, I thanked John for the tour. The experience had left me exhausted and confused. The notion that such a majestic piece of land might have stayed in our family was incomprehensible. I agonized to think that it could still have been ours if not for my grandfather's obstinate pride. It was a lost lottery ticket. A fumbled fourth-down pass. My mother coped with her many painful memories by stifling them, sometimes with the aid of alcohol. She never appeared to be caught by this riptide of regret; I was close to drowning in it.

— EPILOGUE —

How the Ranch Was Lost

TWO YEARS AFTER VISITING Rancho San Carlos, I went to see Uncle David at his winter home in Florida. By then I had pretty much finished excavating the archival record of my grandfather's life, and I wanted to debrief my aging uncle before it was too late. He was eighty-six years old, about the same age as my grandfather had been when I had last seen him. When David greeted me at the door, I was astonished to see how closely he resembled his father. He had the same fleshy earlobes, milky blue eyes, and thin gray hair combed across his freckled, dandruff-flecked scalp.

David and my mother had been estranged for many years on account of his ultra-conservative political views and his nasty alcohol-fueled diatribes. He knew that my parents were Kennedy Democrats and it drove him crazy. He had often telephoned my mother after an evening of heavy drinking to pick a fight with her about Jews and Commies and welfare cheats. When I arrived at his house in Florida, I had barely gotten my suitcase in the door before he began haranguing me about Massachusetts liberals. I did my best to dodge his punches and steer our conversation toward his father.

I spent several days with David and his second wife, Betty, talking about the family and what he remembered about early days at Rancho San Carlos. The last evening of my visit, David asked me, "Do you know the *real* story of how Daddy lost the ranch?" He had just uncorked a bottle of cheap California red wine and poured us each a generous glass. Fox News on a giant screen hummed in the background. "I think I know the story," I said. I proceeded to summarize my mother's account about her father being too proud to accept Esther's offer to pay off the mortgage.

"No, she had it all wrong," David told me, shaking his head. He paused for a minute, as if to create heightened anticipation for what he was about to tell me. Yes, he said, it was true that Esther had offered Moore the money to pay off the mortgage. But she'd added an important condition, namely, that he put the property in both their names. "Your grandmother was a practical woman," he said. He sat up straight and fixed his bloodshot eyes on me. "Well, he took the money, all right. But he never gave it to the bank and he never changed the deed. He screwed everybody and ran off to Los Angeles. When the sheriff came to foreclose on the ranch, the son-of-a-bitch was already gone."

David seemed perversely pleased to drop this bombshell on me. He knew he wasn't going to disabuse me of my Lefty political views, but at least he could persuade me that my grandfather had been thoroughly despicable. My initial response was, "That's impossible!" I immediately wondered if my mother had known this version of the "lost ranch" story. If she did, she never let on. I wanted so much to believe that my grandfather's pride had caused him to reject his ex-wife's offer to pay off the mortgage. Although that scenario was painful to contemplate, at least it preserved for my grandfather a measure of honor and dignity. I could accept that he was a romantic but impractical fool, but not that he was a callous, self-serving thief who would do such a ruinous thing to himself and his family.

I needed no convincing that my grandfather was a crook. In following his sketchy paper trail through the years I had found numerous lawsuits alleging fraud and deceit. He had raised a lot of capital from investors by promising forests full of timber, mines overflowing with minerals, oilfields spewing crude by the tankful. In many cases, these promises never materialized, and investors were left high and dry. It's easy to see Moore as a con artist without a conscience. He seemed to care nothing about the victims of his fraud. David described his behavior as "amoral, not immoral." But how "moral" were the vast fortunes of the Gilded Age, built on unethical monopolistic schemes and on the backs of underpaid laborers? My grandfather certainly was not alone in his dubious business practices.

I should have found my grandfather's conduct reprehensible, as many other people did. As a lawyer in New York City in the 1980s, I helped defend some of the white-collar criminals that Rudy Giuliani, then U.S. Attorney for the Southern District of New York, marched out of their offices in handcuffs to great public fanfare. These people seemed to think that the only thing they'd done wrong was to get caught. They felt entitled to do what they did; if they felt any remorse, they didn't show it. I think my grandfather had the same cavalier attitude about his own unlawful conduct. After all, when my father admonished him about his corrupt business practices, he scoffed at the idea that anyone would put an eighty-six-year old man in jail.

But despite his dubious schemes, I continue to marvel at the scale of my grandfather's endeavors, crooked or not. He succeeded in transforming himself from a low-born immigrants' son into a celebrated international financier who lived the American Dream. He had a true gift for befriending influential people and insinuating himself into their lives. He had boundless optimism for the future and his own good fortune. And if just one of those mining operations had worked out, he would have been living in a Beverly Hills mansion instead of a small apartment in a run-down part of Hollywood. Like so many overnight millionaires, he would have been a society big shot once again.

I find myself identifying with Nick Carraway, who had a similarly paradoxical attitude toward Jay Gatsby. Carraway, with his morally rigorous Midwestern upbringing, declares that Gatsby "represented everything for which I have an unaffected scorn." And yet, although Carraway disdains Gatsby for his gangster ways, he can't help but admire his "romantic readiness," which sets him apart from the "foul dust that floated on the wake of his dreams." Toward the end of the book, Carraway shouts across the lawn to Gatsby, "They're a rotten crowd. You're worth the whole damn bunch put together." Reflecting on this exclamation, Nick writes, "I've always been glad I said that. It was the only compliment I ever gave him, because I disapproved of him from beginning to end."

The last vestiges of my grandfather's messy, flamboyant life have mostly disappeared. I don't know what happened to the jar of Mojave Desert sand. For me, it had long since shed its talismanic power and simply represented the last-ditch hope of a proud man. But the photograph titled "Great Polo Players at Del Monte" hangs over the table where I write. As a child, I had always seen the picture as a symbol of my grandfather's erstwhile eminence in the world. Looking at it now, I get a different sense of him. He seems disengaged from the casually posed group. While his teammates face the camera with satisfaction and pride, he looks shyly away. The expression on his rugged, noble face is pensive, ill at ease. His features are broader and coarser than the other men's; he lacks their slender patrician refinement. He is visibly older, too. His body appears softer and less angular than those of his teammates; his wrinkled neck sags with the gravity of middle age. He stands with his elbows resting behind him so that his jacket is stretched tight across his chest and appears unfashionably short. By contrast, the other men's perfectly fitted jackets hang with casual elegance, as if displayed for a haberdasher's catalog. The picture seems to suggest that although George Moore associated with these men, he was not truly one of them. His money could buy some things, including the opportunity to stand shoulder to shoulder with American aristocrats, but it couldn't buy admission into that aristocracy. There was no safety net of gentility to catch his fall when his money ran out.

 I remember a tense exchange between my parents that took place one afternoon in the mid-1970s at the horse races in Saratoga Springs, New York. We were sitting with several of their friends in the clubhouse. Someone mentioned that Averell Harriman was in the row behind us. My father, no doubt remembering the photograph of "Great Polo Players at Del Monte," announced that Harriman had been a "great friend of Sheilah's father." He urged my mother to go say hello to him. My mother snapped, "Duffy, don't be ridiculous," and changed the subject. I thought little about this at the time. It just seemed another instance of my father's name-dropping, a habit that had always annoyed my mother.

 Recalling that scene at the races, I think that my mother was responding to something more disturbing than her husband's socially insecure boastfulness. I now believe that Harriman's presence triggered my mother's profound ambivalence about her father. She knew better than anyone how perplexing and shape-shifting he was. She knew that he had accomplished many extraordinary things in his life. His brilliance, charisma, and fearlessness had given him entrée into the British aristocracy, Fitzgerald's Jazz Age society, and the highest reaches of American government. But the man she knew as her father was not so grand. His marriages had ended badly; he had lost his fortune and with it his beloved Rancho San Carlos. As if his personal failures weren't enough to diminish him in her eyes, she had to reckon with the fact that he was widely known to have been a remorseless crook who stole his investors' money. Given how my grandfather's life had turned out, to approach Averell Harriman would have mortified her.

As I ponder the grainy image of my grandfather's polo team, I am reminded of the photograph of Gatsby at Oxford, cricket bat in hand, with "half a dozen young men in blazers loafing in an archway." Gatsby shows the photograph to Carraway along with his medal of valor from Montenegro to substantiate the truth of the story he is telling about his life. The photograph seems to prove that he was an "Oxford man," as comfortable on the cricket pitch as he was in the Bodleian Library. But is he really the person he appears to be in the picture? Throughout the book, Carraway—and everyone else—struggles to figure out who Gatsby really is. Both my grandfather's and Gatsby's origins were the subject of much gossip and speculation. Where had they come from and how had they gotten so rich? The photographs of my grandfather and of Gatsby seem to signify unqualified status and belonging. But did the two men truly belong in such company or were they acting a part? In both cases, the pictures suggest deeper veins of truth to be mined.

George Gordon Moore and Jay Gatsby: I keep coming back to this pairing. Ultimately, the two lives—one real, one fictional—were bound by the social caste into which they were born. Despite Gatsby's best efforts to win Daisy's love, he could never remake himself into an upper-class gentleman. During the showdown at the Plaza Hotel, Tom Buchanan called him "Mr. Nobody from Nowhere." Ten years earlier, when Moore was affecting the manner of a London aristocrat, a British newspaper editor referred to him as an "American from Nowhere." Like Gatsby, Moore lacked the credentials to be part of a rarified social sphere in which a distinguished pedigree was the sine qua non for membership. No matter how much money or power he had, he could never truly belong.

When I began to work on this book, I hoped to fill out the life that stood between those emblematic bookends, the polo photograph and the mysterious jar of sand. Some of my questions now have answers; others remain unsettled. Who knows how my grandfather actually lost Rancho San Carlos? Do I believe my mother's story or David's? They were both unreliable narrators, too emotionally invested in the answer to be trusted. My mother chose to believe that her father was a romantic fool. David pegged him as a conniving thief. My grandfather loved land more than anything. And that tips the scale in favor of my mother's account. But I also know that he ran up enormous debt and defrauded many people over the years. So perhaps David was right about him after all. My grandfather was a complicated man. I waver between the two conflicting stories, each freighted with deep-seated bias. But whether he lost the ranch out of pride or avarice, he chose to let it go. And that loss reverberated throughout the lives of his children and grandchildren. To this day, I don't know whose story to believe. But in my confusion and dismay upon hearing David's story, I knew I needed to write this book.

As for the Gatsby mystery, I found a boatload of circumstantial evidence suggesting that Fitzgerald borrowed details from my grandfather's experiences to shape the iconic Jay Gatsby. Editors and friends have sometimes urged me to be less legalistic in my writing, more willing to put my thumb on the scales to make a juicier story. It's tempting to just say "case closed." But that's not how I think. I began this inquiry naively believing that I would find the truth about Fitzgerald and my grandfather. What I've found instead is a deeper understanding of my grandfather. *The Great Gatsby* was the key that opened the door to my grandfather's paradoxes. The novel helped me appreciate the enthusiastic confidence that infused his life, despite his failures and shortcomings. I can't help but think of Nick Carraway's unflagging admiration for Jay Gatsby. As he put it, "There was something gorgeous about him, some heightened sensitivity to the promises of life, as if he were related to one of those intricate machines that register earthquakes ten thousand miles away. . . . [I]t was an extraordinary gift for hope, a romantic readiness such as I have never found in any other person and which it is not likely I shall ever find again." Like Gatsby, my grandfather had an insatiable hunger for the next big chance.

Moore's enthusiasms enabled him to take pleasure in life, no matter what the circumstances, and to share that pleasure with many people. The legendary *New York Times* journalist and three-time Pulitzer prize-winner Arthur Krock, who often attended my grandfather's parties in New York, admired this quality in him. Late in his life, Krock gave my grandfather a book he had written, inscribed "To the only complete Epicurean I have known, who at the same time managed to give others the same enjoyment of life that he has—insofar as they had the capability."

Neither Sonia nor my mother arranged a funeral for my grandfather. But what if, like Gatsby, my grandfather had had a funeral? Would it have been tragically unattended, as Gatsby's had been? I recalled Nick Carraway's disappointment when no one except the minister came to Gatsby's house. When the owl-eyed man, a party guest whom Nick had met in Gatsby's library, showed up at the cemetery, Nick told him that no one had come to the house. The owl-eyed man exclaimed, "Why, my God! They used to go there by the hundreds. The poor son-of-a-bitch." I like to think that some of my grandfather's friends would have taken the trouble to attend his funeral. Surely Countess Sonia would have been there. Would anyone have delivered a eulogy? Who among them would have been up to the task of speaking honestly yet affectionately about him? He wasn't an easy person to understand or to love. It's hard to take the measure of a man who lived so long and so tumultuously, bringing enormous joy to some while wreaking havoc for others.

What if I had been tasked with eulogizing my grandfather? How would I have put together the pieces of his fractured life for a group of his friends who had known him only after his fall from grace? For many years he had been a truly brilliant and successful man who knew how to get things done and to get what he wanted. He had a remarkable ability to comprehend social, financial, and political currents. His audacious maneuvers in World War I helped save many lives. But regardless of those achievements, what distinguished him in my mind was the exaggerated quality of his actions, the amplitude of his passions, and his undying hope for the future. What word could sum up these traits? I suspect that F. Scott Fitzgerald gave a lot of attention to the adjective "great" in the book's title. It suggests many things about Jay Gatsby without tipping the author's hand. Great might refer to his public persona—debonair, wealthy, and popular with the "in" crowd. It also implies theatricality—the artifice with which he invents himself. The word can be taken as ironic—he's nothing but a low-life criminal. Or it might reflect his remarkable capacity to pursue his "incorruptible dream." Looking at my grandfather's life, I believe that he satisfied all these definitions of greatness, just as Gatsby did.

Acknowledgments

This book would not have been possible without the exhaustive and painstaking research of my cousin Steven Moore, the great-great grandson of my grandfather's oldest brother, Thomas Orville Moore. Over the course of many years, Steven put together a family genealogy that traced all the descendants of Ruth Blair Moore and David Moore and their spouses, more than 130 people in all. He collected many thousands of records, including newspaper articles, book excerpts, census data, passport applications, and other information, and organized them in researchable database.

I also owe enormous gratitude to Mark Hugh Miller, author of the *History of Rancho San Carlos* (2018), which traces the history of the ranch from its beginnings in 1834 to 1990, when the Santa Lucia Preserve was created. Mark wholeheartedly supported my work and generously shared his own research with me. Tom Gray, one of the founders of the Santa Lucia Preserve, and Caleb Rosenberg, marketing and communications manager at the Preserve, provided me with photographs from the Preserve's files.

Many friends gave me help and encouragement during the years I spent putting the book together. Ed and Libby Klekowski, Carol Clark, the late Richard Todd, Doug Bauer, Susan Rieger, Margaret Dulaney, Deb Gorlin, Susan Faludi, Russ Rymer, Robert Hammel, and Sven Birkerts helped me figure out what kind of book I was writing. Kitty Florey read through countless drafts over the course of the book's long, slow journey to completion. David Michaelis gave my close-to-final manuscript a thorough and thoughtful reading and cheered me across the finish line.

I am grateful to my cousin David Moore and his wife, Teddy, for their assistance in tracking down family photographs. Diana Fish, the widow of my step-uncle Stuyvesant Fish, took the time to reach out to me with some fascinating information I had known nothing about.

I also owe thanks to everyone in Robbinsville, North Carolina, who opened their doors to me. Carolyn Stewart put me in touch with Cotton McGuire's family and arranged for me to visit Hooper Bald with her brother-in-law, Rev. Daniel Stewart.

Finally, I could never have written this book without the advice, patience, and laser-sharp editing skills of my husband, Chris Benfey, and the enthusiastic curiosity of our sons, Tommy and Nicholas.

Some of my research about my grandfather's experience in World War I appeared in different form in *World War One Illustrated*, Spring 2020, No. 12. Some of my research about Hooper Bald appeared in different form in *Our State* magazine (Oct. 2023).

Notes on Sources

Chapter 1: Dauntless Centaurs

Information about Tommy Hitchcock's early life and service in World War I comes from Nelson W. Aldrich Jr.'s *Tommy Hitchcock, An American Hero* (Fleet Street Corp., 1984), 17–119. Information about Moore and Hitchcock's relationship in New York comes from Aldrich, 121–54. I found Will Rogers's quote about polo in Stephen Zimmer, "Will Rogers and His Horses," National Ranching Heritage Center, Texas Tech University, Feb. 9, 2022. Horace A. Laffaye, *A History of Polo in the United States* (Jefferson, N.C., and London: McFarland & Co., 2011) provides a good overview of the sport's development in this country.

Chapter 2: The Real Gatsby?

Information about Moore's time in New York after World War I comes from Aldrich, 161–82 (see ch. 1 notes). I spoke with Hitchcock's son Billy (William Mellon Hitchcock) on the telephone several times in 2016. He provided interesting details about his parents' relationship with Scott and Zelda Fitzgerald. Information about Moore's friendship with Averell Harriman comes from Rudy Abramson's *Spanning the Century, The Life of W. Averell Harriman, 1891–1986*

(New York: William Morrow and Co., 1992), 167–74. Mary Colum's descriptions of Moore's New York parties are from her memoir, *Life and the Dream* (New York: Doubleday and Co., 1947), 368–71. For biographical information about F. Scott Fitzgerald, I relied primarily on *Scott Fitzgerald*, Andrew Turnbull (New York: Scribner, 1962). For information about scholarly research regarding Fitzgerald's model for Jay Gatsby, I relied primarily on *F. Scott Fitzgerald: A Critical Portrait*, Henry Dan Piper (New York: Holt, Rinehart and Winston, 1965), 112–24; *A Rabble of Dead Money: The Great Crash and the Global Depression: 1929–1939*, Charles R. Morris (New York: PublicAffairs, 2017), 21. I am especially grateful to Mark Hugh Miller for his insightful analysis of competing scholarly theories about the "real" Jay Gatsby in his *History of Rancho San Carlos* (Carmel, CA: Chamisal Press, 2018), 249–304.

Chapter 3: Wyoming

I found much of the information about Moore's early life in the Moore Family Genealogy compiled by Steven Moore, my first cousin thrice removed. His compilation of information about my grandfather contains more than 2,000 documents, including articles from dozens of American and British newspapers and magazines, passenger lists, government records, and histories, memoirs, and biographies in which he is mentioned. Information about Wyoming and the Moore family comes from a Moore family history that was written in two hand-bound volumes by Hilda Canton, George Moore's great-niece. Canton distributed copies of her history to Moore family members, including my mother. Information about the history of Wyoming, Ontario, comes from Isla Smith's *A Small Town Affair* (Ontario: Advertiser Topic, 1971).

Notes on Sources

Chapter 4: Gaining Traction

Hilda Canton's Moore family history includes a brief autobiography that George Moore sent to her in 1968 in which he discussed his early education and path to becoming an attorney in Michigan. Other information about Moore's legal education and early business career comes from articles in the *Detroit Free Press* and the *Port Huron Times Herald*, 1904–09.

Chapter 5: The Racing Life

The *Detroit Free Press* covered Moore's activities in the breeding and racing world from 1907 to 1920. Moore's breeding and racing endeavors were also covered in many other newspapers, including the *New York Tribune,* the *Sun* (NY), the *Los Angeles Times,* and the *Lexington* (KY) *Herald.*

Chapter 6: "I Discovered England"

The *Financial Review of Reviews,* published by the Investment Registry Ltd., included information about the Investment Registry's investment strategy, known as the Geographical Distribution of Capital. The *Review* was a highly regarded publication in financial circles worldwide. Moore's legal problems are detailed in many newspapers, including the *Chicago Daily Tribune* (Oct. 12, 1910) and the *Saginaw* (MI) *Daily News* (Oct. 5, 1910).

Chapter 7: Hunting Pigs in Paradise

Information about Moore's hunting preserve on Hooper Bald comes from a letter dated Feb. 12, 1963, that Moore wrote to Stuyvesant Fish, the son of my grandmother's fourth and final husband, Sidney Fish.

Chapter 8: Cowboy and Cotton

Further information about Moore and Hooper Bald comes from *The European Wild Boar in North Carolina*, Perry Jones (Raleigh [NC]: North Carolina Wildlife Resources Commission, 1959), and *Valley So Wild: A Folk History,* Alberta and Carson Brewer (Knoxville [TN]: East Tennessee Historical Society, 1975), and the Graham County, NC website.

Chapter 9: London Calling

Moore's twelve-page draft memoir provided much of the information in this chapter. The information about Emilie Grigsby comes from Jonathan Walker, *'The Blue Beast': Power and Passion in the Great War* (Stroud [U.K.]: The History Press, 2012), 73-124. For information about Sir John French, I relied on two biographies: Richard Holmes, *The Little Field Marshall, A Life of Sir John French* (London: Jonathan Cape, 1981), and George H. Cassar, *The Tragedy of Sir John French* (Newark: University of Delaware Press, 1985). The description of Moore's parties at Lancaster Gate comes from Will Irwin's autobiography, *The Making of a Reporter* (New York: G. P. Putnam's Sons, 1942), 256–57. Information regarding Moore's hiring of Guy Charteris comes from *A Family Record,* a history of the Wemyss family from the late 19th to early 20th century, by Mary Constance Wemyss Charteris Douglas (the Duchess of Wemyss) (London: Curwen Press, 1932), and correspondence in the Stanway House archives, including a letter from Edward Archibald Hume to R.W. Raper dated Feb. 1, 1910.

Chapter 10: Looks, Bloodlines, and Money

Philip Ziegler's biography, *Diana Cooper* (London: Hamish Hamilton, 1981), provided much of the information about

Diana Manners Cooper and her family. Information also comes from Diana Cooper's autobiography, first published by Rupert Hart-David Ltd. in three separate books: *The Rainbow Comes and Goes* (1958), *The Light of Common Day* (1959), and *Trumpets from the Steep* (1960). A one-volume edition was published by Michael Russell (Publishing) Ltd., Wilton (U.K.) in 1979.

Chapter 11: "War is Certain. Come at Once."

I found information about Moore's early experiences at G.H.Q. in several sources, including Moore's memoir; Irwin's autobiography (see ch. 9 notes); Valentine Williams, *The World of Action* (London: Hamish Hamilton, 1938); Holmes (see ch. 9 notes). Information about the weapons shortage comes from Sir John French's wartime memoir, *1914* (London: Constable and Co. Ltd., 1919); Holmes (see ch. 9 notes); *At G.H.Q.*, (London: Cassell & Co. Ltd., 1931), a collection of diaries and letters written by Brigadier-General John Charteris, who served as Chief of Intelligence at the British Expeditionary Force General Headquarters from 1915 to 1918. French's most personal observations come from his letters to his lover, Winifred Bennett, in the collection of Sir John French's correspondence at the Imperial War Museum in London.

Chapter 12: A Mother's Meddling

My source for the information in this chapter is Catherine Bailey's *The Secret Rooms* (New York: Penguin Books, 2013), 289–410, and a meeting I had with Bailey in London in 2015.

Chapter 13: Dances of Death

The information in this chapter comes from Diana Cooper's autobiography, 95–97, 133–34, 143–46, 150–51, and Ziegler, 61–64 (see ch. 10 notes for these sources).

Chapter 14: A Fog of Ignorance and Doubt

I found information about breaking the press ban and the Shells Scandal in many sources, including Moore's own memoir. Other firsthand accounts came from Irwin's autobiography (see ch. 9 notes), 240–97; Will Irwin, "The English Way," *Metropolitan*, July/Aug. 1915; Williams's autobiography (see ch. 11 notes), 240–66; and French's memoir (see ch. 11 notes), 347–361. Burton J. Hendrick, *Life and Letters of Walter Hines Page* (Garden City [NY]: Doubleday, 1922), gives the perspective of Hines, who served as American ambassador to Great Britain from 1913 to 1918. Hines was strongly in favor of the United States entering the war, a stand that put him at odds with President Woodrow Wilson, a close personal friend of his. Other sources of information include Cassar (see ch. 9 notes), 238–48; Holmes (see ch. 9 notes), 272–313; J. Lee Thompson, *Politicians, the Press, and Propaganda: Lord Northcliffe and the Great War, 1914–1919* (Kent [OH]: Kent State University Press, 1999), 26–65; William G. Shepherd, "The Great Secret: How a Newspaper Reporter from St. Paul Helped Decide the Fate of the British Empire," *Collier's: The National Weekly*, Sept. 13, 1919. For general information about press involvement in World War I, see Martin Gilbert, *The First World War: A Complete History* (New York: Henry Holt & Co., 1994).

Chapter 15: A German Spy at GHQ?

Articles suggesting that Moore was spying for the Germans include West F. de Wend-Fenton, "The Famous Intrigue Against Lord Kitchener," *London Weekly World*, May 18, 1915; de Wend-Fenton, "The Strange Story of Mr. George Gordon Moore," *London Weekly World*, Jan. 26, 1916; "Sir John French Under a Cloud," *New York Times Magazine*, July 4, 1915 (under the byline "A Veteran Diplomat"); "The New Achille and His Patrocles," *The Vital Issue*, July 10, 1915. *The Vital Issue* was an American pro-German weekly newspaper. An account of the libel trial and a partial transcript were published in the London *Times*, March 3, 1916. Moore's controversial interview with the *Detroit Free Press* was published June 27, 1915. Moore's address to the VFW in August 1915 was published in the *New York Times*, Aug. 18, 1915. Information about French's resignation comes from Holmes (see ch. 9 notes), 204, 307–13. Billy Hitchcock told me about Moore's offer to Tommy Hitchcock in a 2016 telephone call.

Chapter 16: "I Always Fear What Too Many Know"

I found information about Moore's stateside involvement in the war in Moore's memoir; diaries and letters in the Edward Mandell House papers at Yale University Library; Charles Seymour, *The Intimate Papers of Colonel House* (New York: Houghton Mifflin Co., 1928), 18–19; Arthur S. Link, ed., *The Papers of Woodrow Wilson*, Vol. 42, April 7–June 23, 1917 (Princeton: Princeton University Press, 1983); Frederick Palmer, *Bliss, Peacemaker* (Palmer Press, 2007), 152–154. Transatlantic crossings between New York and Liverpool during the war years were covered in many newspapers including the *Detroit Free Press*, the *New York Herald*, and the *Evening Telegram* (NY).

Chapter 17: Reckonings

Jean Sifton's memoir was published in the *Pittsburgh Press*, March 8, 1925. An internal investigation at the Investment Registry is referred to in a draft letter from Lord Elcho, a trustee of the Registry, to an unidentified London newspaper editor, in the Stanway House archives. That investigation was criticized as biased and incomplete in the *London Daily News*, July 4, 1911. The *Sporting Times* piece was published Jan. 29, 1916. The details of the Investment Registry's lawsuit against Moore can be found in the court papers filed in *Investment Registry, Ltd. v. Robert Morrison, Jr. and George G. Moore (S.D.N.Y., 1918–19)*. The case was presided over by Judge Learned Hand, one of the most distinguished jurists of the 20th century.

Moore's divorce was covered by several newspapers including the *Detroit Free Press* (Oct. 19, Oct. 23, 1918). Information about Diana's marriage to Alfred Duff Cooper comes from Ziegler (see ch. 10 notes), 101–27. Moore's time in Ireland was described in Holmes (see ch. 9 notes), 339–49. French's appointment of Moore is the subject of a letter dated Aug. 21, 1918, from Sir John French to Lieutenant Colonel Brinsley Fitzgerald in the collection of Sir John French's correspondence at the Imperial War Museum, London.

Chapter 18: The Governor's Daughter

I learned about the Esther Foss-Albert Hickman divorce and Esther's subsequent marriage to George Gordon Moore from Ruth Blair "Winky" Sperber, my maternal half-aunt, with whom I had several telephone conversations in October 2011. Eugene Noble Foss's political career was fascinating. Despite his aggressively pro-business stance, he was a social progressive, introducing Workers' Compensation and advocating for prison and mental health reform. Information about Foss is contained in newspaper articles from 1909 to

1939, mainly in the *Boston Globe* and the *Boston Post*, housed in the Foss Archives in the State Library of Massachusetts. Additional information about Foss comes from Richard Abrams's *Conservatism in a Progressive Era* (Cambridge: Harvard University Press, 1964). Information about Benjamin Sturtevant comes from "Benjamin Franklin Sturtevant, Inventor and Industrialist," Jamaica Plain Historical Society, 2003, and his obituary in the *Boston Globe*, April 18, 1890.

Chapter 19: The Golden State

Articles about the attachment of the San Mateo Polo Club were published on May 5, 1922, in numerous papers, including the *Oakland Tribune*, the *Evening World* (NY), and the *New York Evening Post*. The lawsuit against Moore for unpaid rent was reported in the *San Francisco Chronicle*, Aug. 31, 1922. Information about Moore's acquisition of Rancho San Carlos comes from *History of Rancho San Carlos* (see ch. 2 notes), 303–12. The takeover of the Circle Bar Ranch by Mexican Agraristas was reported in the *Oakland Tribune*, Sept. 23, 1931, and the *Dallas Morning News*, Sept. 26, 1931.

Chapter 20: Stanway on the Pacific

Information about Diana Manners Cooper's visit to Rancho San Carlos comes from her autobiography (see ch. 10 notes), 250–251, 309–12; *San Mateo Times*, Jan. 10, 1927; letter from Diana to Duff dated Jan. 8, 1927, in Artemis Cooper, ed., *A Durable Fire, The Letters of Duff and Diana Cooper 1913–1950* (London: Hamish Hamilton Ltd., 1985), 245.

Robert Louis Stevenson's adventure on the ranch is recounted in "Robert Louis Stevenson and the Goat Ranchers of Carmel Valley," Lindy Perez, The Robert Louis Stevenson Club of Monterey, 2017. Information about Moore's hospitality comes from several newspapers including the *Oakland Tribune* and the *San Francisco Chronicle* as well as the *History of Rancho San Carlos* (see ch. 2 notes), 318–25.

Chapter 21: A 23,000-Acre Playground

Information about Moore's polo playing comes from Aldrich, (see ch. 1 notes), 196–98, and articles in the *San Francisco Chronicle,* the *Los Angeles Times,* the *San Mateo Times,* and other newspapers. *Game and Gossip,* a Monterey Peninsula magazine, also covered local polo. Information about the 1924 Olympics comes from Aldrich, 167–69; and "Polo Team Named for the Olympics," *New York Times,* Mar. 25, 1924. An article about Moore's mounted archery was published in the *Tampa Tribune,* Apr. 25, 1926. Diana's description of Moore's paper chase comes from her autobiography (see ch. 10 notes), 310. Robert Baden-Powell wrote about pigsticking in his *Lessons from the Varsity of Life* (London: C. Arthur Pearson Ltd., 1934). Lt.-Col. Arthur Brooke's essay on pigsticking was published in *Horsemanship, The Way of Man with A Horse,* Maj.-Gen. Geoffrey Brooke (Philadelphia: J. B. Lippincott Co., 1929). Information about boars at the ranch comes from Moore's 1963 letter to Stuyvesant Fish. Moore's boar hunts were written about in several newspaper articles including "Ranch Sports Now Include Boar Hunt," *Amarillo Globe-Times,* May 25, 1937; and *Reno Evening Gazette,* May 5, 1937.

Chapter 22: Empty Promises

The conversation between Bill Wellman and Tommy Hitchcock is reported in Aldrich, 201–02 (see ch. 1 notes). The "fake" oil well lawsuit was reported in *Kokomo Daily Tribune,* Jan. 11, 1929.

Chapter 23: Childhood at Rancho San Carlos
No notes.

Chapter 24: The Foss Twins Behaving Badly

The Moore divorce was reported on April 4, 1933, in the *New York Times,* the *Los Angeles Times,* the *Oakland Tribune,* the *Boston Globe,* and other newspapers. Information about Aidan Roark and Darryl Zanuck comes from Leonard Mosley, *Zanuck: The Rise and Fall of Hollywood's Last Tycoon* (New York: Little Brown & Co., 1984), 143–44, 184–85. Details of the judicial hearing of Esther Moore's divorce complaint against Aidan Roark were reported in the *Los Angeles Times,* Dec. 23, 1937. Una Jeffers wrote about the divorce in a letter to Blanche Matthias, Jan 10, 1939, in *The Collected Letters of Robinson Jeffers with Selected Letters of Una Jeffers, Vol. 2: 1931–1939* (Stanford: Stanford University Press, 2011).

Chapter 25: Decline and Fall

In a 2016 telephone conversation I had with Billy Hitchcock, he recounted his mother's description of Moore's infamous New York dinner party. Carol Baudouin's account of life on the ranch comes from "Woman Recalls Hard Times at Rancho San Carlos" in the Carmel Valley *Weekly Sun,* March 26, 1992. Information about Moore's final years at the ranch comes from Una Jeffers's letters to Mabel Dodge Luhan, July 13, 1932; June 2, 1933; Sept. 7, 1933; Oct. 19, 1933; March 5, 1939; June 21, 1939; Una Jeffers's letters to Phoebe Barkan, Jan. 10, 1933; March 30, 1937; Una Jeffers's letter to Sara Bard Field, Oct. 11, 1931; Una Jeffers's letter to Bennett Cerf, Jan. 1, 1936; Una Jeffers's letter to the Call family, Sept. 12, 1937; Jeffers's letters (see ch. 24 notes). Information about the Hastings at the ranch comes from Una Jeffers's letter to Sara Bard Field, Oct. 11, 1931, and Selina Hastings, *The Red*

Earl, The Extraordinary Life of the 16th Earl of Huntington (London: Bloomsbury, 2014), 104–15.

Chapter 26: "My Easter Holidays"

Information about Martha Finley, author of the *Elsie Dinsmore* series, comes from womenhistoryblog.com. *Elsie's Holiday at Roselands* (New York: Dodd, Mead & Co., 1868) tells the story of Elsie's childhood years.

Chapter 27: Orphans

No notes.

Chapter 28: Out Stealing Horses

Esther Roark's marriage to Sidney Fish was reported on Jan. 10, 1939, in several newspapers including the *Boston Globe* and the *San Francisco Examiner*. My mother's brother, David Moore, told me the story about taking the last horses from Rancho San Carlos to the Fish ranch. Princess Margaret's 1965 visit to the Fish ranch was reported in the *Oakland Tribune*, Nov. 7, 1965.

Chapter 29: Ending Up

Letters between Moore and Harriman dated Aug. 12, 1963; May 22, 1967; and May 24, 1967, are included in W. Averell Harriman papers, Library of Congress, Washington, D.C. Correspondence between George Moore, David Moore, and my father, as well as a copy of Moore's letter to John Lewis dated Nov. 28, 1964, are in my father's legal files.

Chapter 30: Rancho San Carlos Revisited

Information about the history of the ranch after 1940 comes from *History of Rancho San Carlos* (see ch. 2 notes), 357.

Illustration Credits

Cover Julian P. Graham Collection/Loon Hill Studios
iv.   Family photo
vii. Julian P. Graham Collection/Loon Hill Studios
10. Wikimedia Commons
17. Family photo
20. *Our Michigan Friends "As We See 'em"* © Newspaper Cartoonists Association of Michigan, 1905
25. (Top): Courtesy of St. Clair Historical Museum, St. Clair, Michigan
     (Bottom): Family photo
45. Family photo
46. (Top): Courtesy of the McGuire family
     (Bottom): Courtesy of the McGuire family
59. Postcard photographed and published by F. Kehrahn & Co., London, 1905
62. © Philip Halling 2006
67. Bain News Service Collection, Library of Congress
76. H. D. Girdwood Collection, British Museum
96. Alchetron.com

104. Harris & Ewing Collection, Library of Congress
117. *Chicago Eagle*, July 17, 1915
119. The OnLine Books Page, University of Pennsylvania Libraries
126. Bain News Service Collection, Library of Congress
140. *Boston Globe* archives
147. © John Wimberly 1999
151. *Time* magazine archives
152. © David Stoecklein 2007
153. Courtesy of Santa Lucia Preserve
156. Julian P. Graham Collection/Loon Hill Studios
158. Arnold Genthe Collection, Library of Congress
159. Julian P. Graham Collection/Loon Hill Studios
161. Julian P. Graham Collection/Loon Hill Studios
163. Courtesy of Santa Lucia Preserve
170. Courtesy of Santa Lucia Preserve
174. Family photo
175. (Top): Julian P. Graham Collection/Loon Hill Studios (Bottom): Family photo
176. Family photo
179. Family photo
180. Julian P. Graham Collection/Loon Hill Studios
181. Family photo
191. Courtesy of Santa Lucia Preserve
193. Family photos
194. Family photo
196: Family photo

Illustration Credits

198. Courtesy of Santa Lucia Preserve
201. Wikipedia
216. Julian P. Graham Collection/Loon Hill Studios
217. Family photo
224. Family photo

About the Author

MICKEY RATHBUN practiced law in New York City in the 1980s before moving to Western Massachusetts and turning her attention to her true passion, writing. Her hundreds of features and personal essays have appeared in many publications including the *Boston Globe*, the *Chicago Tribune*, and *Salon.com*. For the past six years, she has been the garden columnist for the *Daily Hampshire Gazette* in Northampton, Massachusetts. She lives in Amherst with her husband, writer Christopher Benfey, and their rescue mutt, Luisa.

www.ingramcontent.com/pod-product-compliance
Lightning Source LLC
Chambersburg PA
CBHW051118160426
43195CB00014B/2254